America

by Stephen Vincent Benét

Prose

THE BEGINNING OF WISDOM
YOUNG PEOPLE'S PRIDE
JEAN HUGUENOT
SPANISH BAYONET
JAMES SHORE'S DAUGHTER
THE DEVIL AND DANIEL WEBSTER
THIRTEEN O'CLOCK
JOHNNY PYE AND THE FOOL-KILLER
TALES BEFORE MIDNIGHT

Poetry

FIVE MEN AND POMPEY
TIGER JOY
HEAVENS AND EARTH
JOHN BROWN'S BODY
BALLADS AND POEMS
BURNING CITY
YOUNG ADVENTURE
A BOOK OF AMERICANS
(with Rosemary Benét)
NIGHTMARE AT NOON
THEY BURNED THE BOOKS
WESTERN STAR

Selected Works

VOLUME ONE: POETRY
VOLUME TWO: PROSE

Libretto

THE DEVIL AND DANIEL WEBSTER

Stephen Vincent Benét

America

HOLT, RINEHART AND WINSTON

New York · Chicago · San Francisco

E
178
B43

;9580

Published simultaneously in Canada by Holt, Rinehart and Winston of Canada, Limited.

Published, May, 1944
Twelfth Printing, January 1969

SBN: 03-028535-6
PRINTED IN THE UNITED STATES OF AMERICA

Stephen Vincent Benét often used to say that people of other lands would understand our country better if they could meet us in our own backyard, learn something of our habits and our history, hear what we have to say and see what we stand for.

The Office of War Information suggested in the winter of 1942 that Mr. Benét write a short, interpretive history of the United States for translation into many languages. He gladly went to work and finished the manuscript shortly before his death.

He wrote the book simply, out of his deep love for his country and belief in its free traditions. For that reason we believe his *America* will bring to Americans a reaffirmation of faith in the enduring things of our past and understanding of the high role we must play among the nations of the world.

The Publishers

CONTENTS

America

There is a country of hope, there is a country of freedom. There is a country where all sorts of different people, drawn from every nation in the world, get along together under the same big sky. They go to any church they choose—Catholic, Protestant, Jewish, Mohammedan, Buddhist—and no man may be persecuted there for his religion. The men and women of this country elect the people they wish to govern them, remove those people by vote—not by revolution—if they feel their representatives have done badly, speak their minds about their government and about the running of their country at all times, stay themselves and yet stay loyal to one cause, one country, and one flag.

The flag is the Stars and Stripes. The country is the United States of America. The cause is the cause of democracy.

It is not an earthly paradise, a Garden of Eden, or a perfect state. It does not pretend to be any of those things.

It has not solved every problem of how men and women should live. It has made mistakes in its own affairs, mistakes in the affairs of the world. But it looks to the future always—to a future of free men and women, where there shall be bread and work, security and liberty for the children of mankind.

It does not want to rule the world or set up an American empire in which Americans will be the master race and other people subject races. If you ask any real American whether he believes in a master race, you will get a long stare or a long laugh. Americans do not believe in master races.

It is a fighting country, born in battle, unified in battle, ready and willing always to fight for its deep beliefs. It has never lost a war. But it does not believe that war and the martial spirit are the end and goal of man. It honors the memory of its great soldiers—men like Washington and Grant and Lee—as it honors the names of those who fight for it to-day. But every one of those men fought for something more than conquest. When the wars were done, they said: "Let us have peace. Let us build up the land. Let us make something, build something, grow something that was not there before. Let us try to make a good country—a place where people can live in friendship and neighborliness."

It is a queer country, in some ways. It is young among the nations of the world. But its system of government has endured for over a century and a half, flexible to changed conditions, but without essential change. The thirty-second President of the United States now sits in the White House, the seventy-eighth Congress of the United States is now in session. They were put there by the will of the people. And, since the Constitution of the United States was first adopted, the people have stayed in power and the will of the people has ruled. Always, since the first, the American people have had a chance to use their own judgment, make their own mistakes, correct them and go ahead. And "the people," in America, does not mean a class, a caste, or a specially appointed set of men. It means you and me and the man next door—the butcher, the baker, the farmer, the workman, the lawyer, the doctor, the woman who keeps her house. It means everybody.

Under this sort of government, the United States has become prosperous and wealthy, a huge industrial power, a vast granary of food. Yet, whenever flood or fire, earthquake or catastrophe devastated another land, American food and medical supplies, American nurses and doctors have gone there to help out. They went because they thought they should.

To our enemies, the United States is a country entirely composed of millionaires, gangsters, weaklings, movie stars, corrupt politicians, idle women, and a starved and selfish proletariat. We Americans do not mind their saying any of those things. Our enemies can make no harsher or sterner criticisms of the country we believe in and love than have already been made by loyal and devoted Americans, living and dead.

Behind every American soldier in this war stands the spirit of the country he serves. It may be misinterpreted, forgotten, badly expressed, even betrayed by the individual. But it is there. We do not claim to have put an army of angels in the field. They are average Americans, brought up in freedom, fighting for freedom. That is all. They are tall and short, dark and fair, talkative and silent—men who work with their hands, men who work with their heads—men who come from little towns and big cities and quiet farms—all sorts of men. But behind them all, whether they are able to talk about it or not, there is a spirit. A spirit and an idea.

What is that spirit? What is the American spirit, the American idea?

How did it get started? What made it? What does the United States of America mean—not just as a big rich country that makes a lot of automobiles, radios, iceboxes, movies, and sanitary toilets—but as a living force in the world?

America

Let us look at the record. Let us look at the facts. If you want to find out what a man is really like, you find out about his parents, his family, the house he lives in, the way he was brought up. Let us do that with the United States of America. How did it get started—and why?

The United States began with two small groups of resolute
people fighting a wilderness—one at Jamestown, Virginia, one
at Plymouth, Massachusetts.

They were not the first settlers on the North American
continent—not by over a century. Already the great Spanish
explorers, De Soto, Coronado, Cabeza de Vaca, had landed,
wandered, suffered, brought news of rolling plains and great
rivers and Indian-haunted forests. Already the stubborn fishermen of France had found the Grand Banks. Already Florida
was settled and the coasts of Canada known to brave sailors.
Both St. Augustine in Florida and Santa Fe in New Mexico
are far older towns than either Jamestown or Plymouth. And
yet, it was at those two chance spots on the Atlantic seaboard
that the adventure of the United States began.

Other colonists from England had tried the land and failed.
Raleigh's colony at Roanoke had been swallowed up in the
woods, leaving nothing behind but a name cut on a tree,
"Croatan," and a haunting legend. Now to a low-lying penin-
sula in the wide James River, on May 24, 1607, came three
little nutshells of ships, not for a raid or a foray, but to plant
men in the land.

What sort of men were they? Why did they come? What
sort of laws, customs, habits did they bring from the Old
World to the New World?

They were adventurers. They came looking for gold and

quick profits, as many men have come to many lands. They were sent by a trading company—the Virginia Company—that hoped to make money on the venture. That is true.

But, while they were adventurers, they were not just a military expedition, sent out under martial law. They were sent out as a colony—sent out to build houses and roads and churches, find out what the land was like and how Englishmen could live in it. That is important. Nor were they slaves. They were free men. And that is important, too.

We have the royal charter and the letter of instructions that guided them. There are two important things in those documents.

In the first place, though they were going to the ends of the earth (as people thought of America, then) they were guaranteed "their rights as Englishmen," even at those ends of the earth. They were, by the king of England's word, "to have and enjoy all liberties, franchises and immunities within any of our other dominions, to all intents and purposes as if they had been abiding and born within this our realm of England." In other words, the man who went to Jamestown was to have the same rights as the man who stayed at home. He was not to be wantonly used or tyrannically oppressed. He could appeal to the law. He was to have all the rights of an Englishman living in England.

In the second place, these adventurers in Virginia were to be ruled, in Virginia, by a president and a council that advised the president. No one-man rule.

So they got to Jamestown—one hundred and five of them —and the story is one of heroism, suffering, and hardship. These fresh-faced English people had come to a land as strange to them as the craters and mountains of the moon would be to us today. Everything was new and strange to them—the birds, the beasts, the flowers, the Indians, the heat of the summer, the very taste of the water in the river. They were awed and dazzled, like children. They were homesick, like children. They died of fever, of starvation, by Indian arrows. Sometimes the Indians would fight them, sometimes be friendly. The settlers never knew which would be which or why. At one point, in one year, the few who were still left alive abandoned Jamestown and fled in boats down the river. But at the mouth of the river, in the bay, they met relief ships from England—and went back to Jamestown, to start all over again. That took great courage. But they went back.

Their names were Smith, Percy, Brown, Allcock, Midwinter, Sergeant, Martin. They were seed blown over the water. Many died, a few lived and throve.

They didn't find gold, they didn't make easy money. But, after twelve years of trial, they had made a colony. Women came over; children were born in the town.

On July 30, 1619, in the wooden church at Jamestown, on the edge of nowhere, the first assembly of Virginia met. The governor was there, and his councilors—and twenty-two other men called burgesses and representing eleven different settlements in the colony. They worked together, those hot July days, passing various laws and regulations for the colony itself. Not such very important laws, but necessary to them. Nobody should kill cattle without the governor's permission —cattle were scarce. Anybody who stole a boat from his neighbor or a canoe from the Indians should be punished for it. All ministers, once a year, should bring in a report of the marriages, burials, and christenings they had performed. And so forth. But twenty-two other men, besides the governor and his councilors, had played a part in making those laws. They had met and argued and said what they had to say about their own lives and the way they wanted things done.

No, it wasn't self-government yet—not by any means. But something had begun. Men who had crossed an ocean to fight a wilderness thought they had a right to some say in the way in which they were governed. And the English government admitted that right, as a matter of common sense. In times to come, there were to be many quarrels and difficulties between governor and burgesses. But the burgesses stayed, speaking up for the colony and its interests, and you will hear of them again. The seed of freedom took root in the rich earth, between the rows of tobacco, under the warm Virginia sky.

And, meanwhile, something else had begun to happen, too. When John Pory came over from England, in 1619, to write his account of Virginia, he wrote:

"Our cowekeeper here . . . on Sundays goes accoutered dressed all in freshe flaming silke; and a wife . . . of a collier of Croydon, weares her rough bever hatt with a faire pearl hatband . . ."

That was the other thing.

The New World did not care if a man had been a knight or a cowkeeper, before he came there. If he did well, in the New World, his wife could dress in silk and nobody would think it odd. And that, too, has always been a part of the American dream—that a man should have a chance to do his best and rise in the world—that no man is better than another man because his parents had money or titles or power.

Now let us go north—more than a thousand miles north to a harsher and colder coast—the coast of New England in winter.

The Pilgrims landed there on November 11, 1620, from a ship called the *Mayflower*.

Who were the Pilgrims and why did they come to America? Were they adventurers, conquerors, gold seekers?

No, they were not. A few of those on the *Mayflower* came on the chance of getting land and farms of their own. But most came for another reason. They came because they wished to worship God in their own way—a simple and faithful way, but not the way of the Established Church of the England of their time.

They were family men, for the most part. They brought their wives and their children with them on a 64-day voyage, in a small, tossing ship. One child was born on the voyage, two others just after the landfall. Again, the whole company numbered a little over a hundred human beings. Again, it was backed by an English company whose investors put money into the venture. But the backbone of the venture was this group of quiet, family men, bringing their wives and children to a coast at the world's end.

Why did they do such a crazy thing? Why on earth did they take such a chance? Nobody ordered them to do it, bribed them to do it. They went to great trouble and pain, uprooted their homes, left everything they had known behind, from the memories of childhood to the things in the house that one looks at and cannot take because there will be no room, and yet remembers.

They wanted to worship God in their own way. They were resolved and determined to worship God in their own way.

They had started their long journey in the North of England, many years before—farmers, farm servants, a postmaster, a preacher, a boy who read books late at night. They had refused to worship as the church and the authorities of England said they should worship—and had got into trouble. So they had gone over to Holland and lived quietly and soberly there, for they were hard-working and honest people. But still they hungered for a place of their own, where they could live as they chose. Now, after many years and great labor, they had found such a place, across great seas. And they looked at it and their sober hearts rejoiced.

But, who was to govern them in this new land? How were they to run their affairs?

That takes a little explaining.

The Pilgrims were neither servants, slaves, nor tenants of their moneyed friends in England. They were sharers in a common enterprise. The moneyed man in England put up ten pounds for a share. The Pilgrim who had no money put up himself—his willingness to cross the seas and help build a colony. At the end of seven years, all capital and profits of the colony were to be divided proportionately among these partners. If all went well, each partner would get what he wanted—the moneyed man a profit, the Pilgrim a refuge and a home.

But—and this was important—once they got to America, the Pilgrims meant to govern themselves. And this was agreed to. The merchants in London might counsel and advise, they could not order or command. They could ask questions about profits, give help, send over men. But they could not tell the Pilgrims how to run the affairs of the colony, once that colony was started.

Still there had to be something more than that. The Pilgrims were Englishmen, going overseas—the colony they founded would be an English colony. So, before the Pilgrims sailed, they tried to get some sort of charter or document from King James of England, giving the expedition his official approval.

The King would not give such a promise and they had to do without it. King James let it be known that if the Pilgrims behaved themselves and didn't make trouble, he would let them alone. But that was as far as he would go. He didn't intend to persecute them but he didn't intend to give them his royal blessing.

So, in the end, the Pilgrims sailed with just this much official authorization—a patent, a right to settle, not from the crown but from the Virginia Company. And that would be legal and valid, as long as they settled in Virginia.

But they didn't settle in Virginia, as they had originally intended. They settled in New England. Historians give various reasons for their change of plans. But the simplest explanation is the easiest. They had been sixty-four days in a crowded ship. And now they saw land—solid land. It might not be a paradise, it might not be as fertile and warm as Virginia—but it was land. It was wild and savage land, but they could smell it and touch it and taste it and walk on the solid earth. No wonder that they decided to seek no farther.

Still, once they settled in New England, their patent from the Virginia Company was worthless. The Virginia Company had no rights over New England. And there were men on the *Mayflower*, not Pilgrims, who muttered that now they were outside of all government.

So the Pilgrims and their friends, free men and seekers after God, met in the cabin of the *Mayflower* and drew up a paper. We know it as "The Mayflower Compact." And it said:

"In the name of God, Amen. We, whose names are underwritten, the Loyal Subjects of our dread Sovereign Lord King James, by the Grace of God, of Great Britain, France, and Ireland, King, Defender of the Faith, etc. Having undertaken, for the Glory of God, and Advancement of the Christian Faith, and Honour of our King and Country, a Voyage to plant the first colony in the northern Parts of Virginia; Do by these Presents, solemnly and mutually in the presence of God and one another, covenant and combine ourselves together into a civil Body Politick, for our better Ordering and Preservation, and Furtherance of the Ends aforesaid; And by Virtue hereof do enact, constitute, and frame, such just and equal Laws, Ordinances, Acts, Constitutions, and Offices, from time to time, as shall be thought most meet and convenient for the general Good of the Colony; unto which we promise all due Submission and Obedience. In Witness thereof we have hereunto subscribed our names at Cape Cod the eleventh of November, in the reign of our Sovereign Lord King James of England, France, and Ireland, the eighteenth and of Scotland, the fifty-fourth. Anno Domini 1620."

Forty-one men signed the compact and ratified the choice of John Carver as the first governor of the colony. Then they set about exploring the country and finding a place to live.

What did the compact mean—the compact they signed? Did it mean independence? No, they said they were loyal subjects of the King of England.

Did it mean liberty, equality, democracy for all? No, that was not to come yet.

But words had been said, words had been written down. Men had met together and, of necessity, made a government where no government had been before, a government that should make "just and equal laws . . . for the general good." And, later on, other men were to remember that meeting and that pledge. The thing could be done. Ordinary men—stocking weavers, wool combers, quiet fathers of families—could get together and decide how to run their own affairs, without the help of a charter or a royal order or a set of instructions from a company. They could, and they did, and the memory stayed in men's minds.

Meanwhile, like the first men at Jamestown, the men and women of Plymouth fought hardship and the wilderness. Theirs was an ordeal by cold, instead of an ordeal by heat, but the suffering and the sickness were the same. Half of them died the first winter and were laid to rest in the frosty earth of the new land, where they sleep still. But, though strong men died and gallant women, they saved every child. And when the spring came—the green spring of New England—they found that the birds sang sweetly.

From the Indians they learned how to plant corn, and the uses of corn. They learned how to catch the eels in the river, they learned how to take care of themselves in a savage land. Through the first years, they hung upon the edge of starvation. But, in the end, they did what they had come to do. From the trees of the forest and the resolute iron of their hearts they built an abiding place where they could worship God as they chose.

So another seed was planted in American ground. At Jamestown, men kept the rights they had brought from overseas, found the wilderness made men equal, and set up an assembly. At Plymouth, men asserted and maintained their right to worship God in their own way, and set up a system of local self-government, not all-inclusive, but quite different from the system under which they had been born and brought up. And, in both places, a man had value as a man.

Who were some of those first men?

John Smith, at Jamestown, soldier, explorer, mapmaker, teller of tall stories, bushy-bearded, inquisitive, curious, indefatigable, delighted with all new things, but mapping the coasts of Virginia and New England with a patient pen. William Bradford of Plymouth, self-taught scholar, full of gentleness, full of fortitude, a follower of God, governor of the colony for thirty years, leaving a library of four hundred books when he died. Others, the bad and the good, the stupid and the simple—some criminals, yes—one murderer, even among the Pilgrim company—but, in the main, common men, ordinary men and women, who rose to the new chance they had and made something of it. Farmers, stocking weavers, younger sons, adventurers, carpenters, plowboys—no roll of the rich and the great. A real knight—Sir Richard Saltonstall—came with the next big emigration, the Massachusetts Bay Colony. Other men and women of rank and title were to come later. But, on the whole, the rich and the great, the complacent and the docile, stayed at home. Of those who came, it was said that God winnowed the wheat to plant in the wilderness. And, of how they felt about coming, let Bradford speak: "It was granted the dangers were great but not desperate; the difficulties were many but not invincible." And there was a later saying, when America moved to the western plains: "The cowards never started and the weak died on the way." And, on the whole, that was so, of these first men. It was bound to be so. You do not leave everything you have known behind and cross raging seas in small ships without fortitude, adventurousness, daring, belief in God, desire to be free and a man—some compelling and driving force. And if you bring nothing but emptiness, you do not live. There were rascals who came indeed—no country is without its rascals. But those who lived and survived learned to stand on their own feet. And so it was in the beginning.

THE GREAT MIGRATION

Then they began to come, like bees to a clover field. And, from 1620 on, they kept coming.

It was a vast westward movement, not only from the British Isles but from all Europe. They were drawn to the strange, new world like iron filings to a magnet. They came as individuals; they came in groups and societies and church congregations. They were brought over for special skills, like the Italian glassmakers, who came to Jamestown; they came under hard conditions of labor, as the Greeks and Minorcans were to come to New Smyrna in Florida. They came from many stocks—the Dutch to New Netherlands, the Swedes to Delaware, the French to South Carolina and the vast southern lands that changed hands between France and Spain, the Spaniards to Florida, New Mexico, California, the Irish, Scotch and Germans to Pennsylvania, the English everywhere. And they all brought something. The Swedes, for instance, brought the log cabin—they built the first log cabins anywhere in the American colonies. The Dutch brought many things, among them the saint of good children—St. Nicholas, Santa Claus. The Germans brought their patient ways of farming. The French brought their skill with the vine.

Rebels came—men who had fought for king or common-wealth, and their side lost and they fled to a new land. Re-ligious enthusiasts came—men who, like the Pilgrims, wished to worship God in their own way, without interference. Hungry men came—poor but knotty men who wanted to rise in the world. Men who would take a chance came—men willing to sell the labor of their bodies for a term of years on the chance of getting, at the end, a hat, a suit of clothes, a cheap gun—and opportunity. And there were vagabonds and criminals—yes. There were those.

It was not yet the great melting pot that it later became. It was still predominantly British in stock. But the new names were there—Seixas, De la Noye, Van Cortlandt, Groghan, Mansker, Herkimer—a hundred others. And each new stock, as it came, brought its own traditions, its own tincture, its own flavor to American life.

By 1776, there were thirteen colonies on the Atlantic sea-board, stretching a thousand miles from Maine to Georgia. Thirteen colonies, with perhaps two million people, all under the English flag—and all very different.

They had spread north and south, pushed inland along the routes of the great rivers. They had not yet flooded into the vast mid-section of the country—they were still held back from that by the long mountain wall of the Appalachians, though, at points, the wall had been pierced by hardy settlers.

And the land had been gained by blood, toil, sweat, and fighting, by treaty and by war, by rifle, ax and plow, and by the hope of building something new.

Thirteen colonies, all rather different, each one ruled

somewhat differently, each one with different characteristics. These were the thirteen—each one remembered by a stripe in the Stars and Stripes. The dates are the dates of their first settlement:

Virginia	—1607
New York	—1614
Massachusetts	—1620
New Hampshire	—1623
Maryland	—1634
Connecticut	—1635
Rhode Island	—1636
Delaware	—1638
North Carolina	—1650
New Jersey	—1664
South Carolina	—1670
Pennsylvania	—1682
Georgia	—1733

Of these Virginia and Massachusetts had been founded, as you know, at Jamestown and Plymouth. Rhode Island, the smallest colony, but one of the most independent-minded, had been founded by Roger Williams in 1636 and religious liberty had been guaranteed its inhabitants since 1663. Pennsylvania had been founded by William Penn, a Quaker, and many Quakers had settled there. Georgia had originally been founded by James Oglethorpe as a philanthropic experiment to help poor debtors—imprisonment for debt was a serious problem in the England of his time, and he wanted a place where men could start anew. The Dutch had first founded New York as the New Netherlands colony, and it had become the Province of New York in 1664. Maryland had been founded by a Catholic noble, Lord Baltimore, and Catholic priests and laymen had been among its first settlers. Many different starts and beginnings, as you can see—no one set pattern for all the colonies.

And if, say in 1765, you had asked these colonists just what they were, they would have said, "I'm a Massachusetts man, a Virginia man, a Georgia man." That was how they thought of themselves. They flew the flag of England, they drank the King of England's health. But they were not living in England—there were many now who had never seen England or its shores. The word "American" had been long in use, but it did not mean then what it means today. They were not all part of one big nation. They were Massachusetts men, Connecticut men, Rhode Island men. And the way of the rich Virginia tobacco planter was not the way of the New England farmer or of the pioneer in the wilderness cabin.

And yet, they did have some things in common, these various men, these different colonies. They must have had, or they never would have made a nation at all.

What had they done, what had they accomplished, in the hundred and sixty-odd years since Jamestown?

They had built cities and towns—Philadelphia, Boston, New York, Williamsburg, Charleston. They had pushed the Indian back and rooted themselves in the land. They had cleared forests away and turned the land to grainland and plowland. They had bred bold sailors, shrewd merchants, hardy sea captains. They had certain men of wealth and leisure —men who lived well and thought well of themselves. They had others who owned vast tracts of land and lived in a sort of provincial splendor—untitled lords of plantations and manors and grants. They had schools, colleges, churches, public buildings. Their commerce, even under regulations, throve. They had weavers, dyers, printers, silversmiths, artisans of various kinds. Though farming, tobacco raising, fishing were still the chief occupations. They had industries—indeed there were more iron furnaces and iron forges in the thirteen colonies in 1775 than there were in England and Wales, though most of these furnaces and forges were small ones. If you went to Philadelphia or New York or Boston, you would find theaters, newspapers, concerts, dances, taverns—the various things that make up the web of city life.

But that is not why European travelers were interested in what they found in America. Philadelphia was not Paris, New York was not London—the gay society of the little cities was like any other gay society, only a little behindhand in its fashion and its taste and still looking respectfully to Europe for the right word, the right kind of buttons to wear on a coat, the right tunes to play at a dance. The European travelers had seen finer cities, richer merchants. They had even seen better farming than they found in some parts of the country—for American farming, at the time, tended to be wasteful. There was so much land that a man could clear ground, exhaust it, and move on to somewhere else.

No, it wasn't these material things that the European travelers found interesting. They were used to material things. They found a spacious country, beautiful and strange—but a country whose civilization was still provincial, a country where, beyond the belts of long-settlement, nature still stood up against man like an adversary to be struggled with, wrestled with, not just for a day or a year but every day. What interested them most was the spirit and temper of its people, and the way in which they lived together.

Let us hear from Hector St. John de Crèvecœur, a civi-·lized Frenchman who came to the New York Colony in 1759, and lived there for twenty years and wrote of his experiences.

"We have no princes for whom we toil, starve and bleed —Here man is free as he ought to be . . . What then is the American, the new man? He is either a European or the descendant of a European, hence that strange mixture of blood which you will find in no other country. I could point out to you a family whose grandfather was an Englishman, whose wife was Dutch, whose son married a French woman and whose present four sons have now four wives of different nations. Here individuals of all nations are melted into a new race of men whose labors and posterity will one day cause great changes in the world . . . The American is a new man who acts upon new principles; he must therefore entertain new ideas and form new opinions . . ."

Brave words—enthusiastic words. But what were these new principles? What was this experiment in human living?— for, if European visitors agreed on nothing else, they agreed that there was such an experiment, and one worth watching.

In the first place, without deliberately setting out to do so, the colonies had established the principle that a man's religion is his own affair. You could not say that Quakers should not come to America, when Quakers had settled Pennsylvania. You could not say that Catholics should not come to America, when Catholics had founded Maryland. You could not say that Jews should not come to America, when Jews had settled in Philadelphia, Newport, and elsewhere. You could not say that Protestants should not come to America, when Protestants had begun New England.

It is true that Catholics labored under certain restrictions in certain colonies. But they were not harried for their faith. It is true that, in the beginnings of New England, the New England Puritans had tried to set up a sort of ruling church and had expelled and driven out those who did not agree with them. But they could not make it work. The size of the land was against them. You might drive a man out of your town— that was hard on him. But a hundred, two hundred miles away, he could take up other land, live on it, and worship as he pleased. That very thing happened to Roger Williams, the founder of Rhode Island. Driven out of Massachusetts for his beliefs, he set up another colony where men of all shades of belief could live in harmony together. And, once he had the charter of his colony, the Massachusetts men could do nothing against him. And so it was again and again. There was room for all faiths in the wide land. And, because there was room, they grew and flourished—often side by side.

In the second place, as a man's religion was his own business, so his parentage and where he had come from was his own business, too. Had the colonies been settled entirely by any one nation, things might have been different. But they were not settled that way. The land was hungry for men, and men came from everywhere. The frontier was hungry for men and it did not ask what a man had been before but how good a pioneer he was. No man was shut out because he was blue-eyed, black-eyed, red-haired, yellow-haired, a Jew from Hamburg, an Irishman from Cork, a miner from Wales, a shoemaker from Bristol. And there was opportunity in the colonies for any man of any race.

To this there was one great exception—the Negro slaves We shall talk of that in its place.

In the third place, these men of the colonies had had very considerable practice in self-government. And, again, that was something that the size and character of the land made inevitable. And other things as well.

As we saw, the very first colonists, at Jamestown and Plymouth, brought with them their rights as Englishmen— the same rights they would have had at home in England. They brought with them, too, a knowledge of English government—not a despotism or an absolute monarchy, but a government in which you elected representatives to sit in the House of Commons and help manage the affairs of the nation. And from this English idea of a parliament stemmed the various American colonial assemblies. They were, in a sense, little local parliaments. They didn't have the same powers, of course, but they gave men practice in talking things over, thrashing questions out, deciding what should be done and what shouldn't be done. Some assemblies were stronger, some weaker than others. But, even in a crown colony, a hostile or unwilling assembly could make things very uncomfortable for a royal governor, as many governors found out.

Nor was this all. In New England, where the township was the local unit, the custom of town meeting was very old. And to this town meeting came the citizens of the town to decide on their local officials, their local problems. And here, in these local town meetings, almost everyone had a voice. In early Massachusetts, for instance, you mightn't be what was called a "freeman" and so take part in the larger affairs of the colony. But, even so, you could vote for selectmen, you could serve on a jury, hold office in the militia, and freely present petitions and grievances to the General Court. "Thus, before 1652, when Massachusetts declared herself an independent commonwealth, all men in the colony of mature years who had taken the oath of fidelity, possessed some share in government, whether local or general," says Charles M. Andrews, the historian. Not all colonies had the same system. But, if you take thirty years as a generation and count from 1652, by the time the American Revolution broke out, four generations of Massachusetts men had been used to some share in their own government.

And then there was the frontier—and the million people who lived on the frontier. To the people of the frontier, colonial governors and assemblies were far away, and the rule of England still farther. Engaged in a life-and-death struggle with the wilderness, they had to govern themselves, for nobody else would do it for them. The king of England could not make your clearing. The governor of Virginia could not plant your corn. You had to do these things yourself. And, as soon as other men and women moved into your neighborhood, you had to get along with them. You had to arrange for mutual protection—a log fort, for instance, where the scattered settlers could go in case of Indian attack. If you wanted a church to worship in, you had to build one. All of you. If a man was a thief, a murderer, a nuisance to the community, you had to try him and punish him. All of you. If you wanted a mayor for your log town, a leader for your community, a captain to fight the Indians, you had to get together and choose him. All of you. Just as the Pilgrims chose their first governor.

In time, of course, the regular courts, the regular law officers, the regular governmental system, might come your way. Even so, you were going to have some say in the way things were run, because outsiders might not understand your particular problems. And the frontier did have its say. In Pennsylvania, for instance, the new Scotch-Irish settlers in 1730 seized 15,000 acres of frontier land that technically belonged to the proprietors of the colony. They did so, saying that "it was against the laws of God and nature that so much land should remain idle while so many Christians wanted it to labor on." In North Carolina, the frontiersmen, finding themselves with many complaints against the government of the colony, broke into open revolt in 1770 and fought a pitched battle with government militia in 1771. The frontier was tough and resourceful. It didn't respect riches or titles. It didn't respect long descent or a famous name. It respected hardiness and it wanted its own way. And it was ready to fight for its own rights.

So there you have the colonies in the early 1770's—an experiment in human living—a nation not yet formed—thirteen different little countries, all speaking the same language but not yet unified in heart. There were classes and distinctions. There were rich and poor. But few of the rich had been rich for many generations and most of the poor did not intend to stay poor. Beside the more fixed and rigid societies of Europe and Britain, America was a place where almost anything could happen to almost any man. The frontiersman might be poor, in money and goods, compared to the Boston merchant, but he thought himself as much of a man and more. The New England farmer might not talk much of the rights of man but he knew that he had rights as a man, and he meant to keep them. The member of the Virginia House of Burgesses might not think that everybody should vote, but he believed in representative government. Democracy might be an ugly word in the ears of the Boston merchant, but resistance to autocratic rule was something he understood and approved of. The new immigrant, once acclimated, found himself enough of an American to criticize things he didn't like and strike out for himself in his own way. It didn't matter what he had been, it mattered what he could prove himself to be. That was the American lesson—the American opportunity—seeing what would happen to a man once he was treated as a man. And Americans believed in that—and they still do.

Of course, they didn't write it all down on paper, as a set of rules. They were still groping, striving, living from day to day. They did have certain examples of what Americans could be and do—and what this sort of treatment did for them. They had, for instance, the example of Benjamin Franklin.

Franklin was born in Boston in 1706—the tenth son of a tallow chandler and soap boiler named Josiah Franklin. A bright youngster, he learned to read early, but left school at ten to help in his father's business. At twelve, he became an apprentice-printer, under his brother James. At seventeen, still a printer, he moved to Philadelphia. By the time he was twenty-three, he was running his own newspaper successfully. And from then on, there were few things that he did not do.

He wrote and published *Poor Richard's Almanac*, full of common sense, humorous, pithy maxims that people still like to read. He invented the lightning rod. He laid the foundations for the science of electricity. He taught himself French, Italian, Spanish, and Latin. He printed the first novel ever printed on an American printing press. He established the first circulating library in Philadelphia and organized the first police and fire companies in the colonies. He was postmaster general of North America. He was unofficial ambassador from the colonies to England. Before he died, he was to be a member of every learned society in Europe, a diplomat, a scientist, a philosopher, and one of the most talked-about men in the world.

Strong, healthy, humorous, unpretentious, wise, this son of struggling parents, coming late to a crowded family, won world-wide fame. Yet he always called himself "Benjamin Franklin, Printer" and in one of his last letters he said, with full conviction: "God grant that not only the love of liberty but a thorough knowledge of the rights of man may pervade all the nations of the earth, so that a philosopher may set his foot anywhere on its surface and say 'This is my country.'"

That is what he hoped, that is what he thought and worked for. He was a genius, yes—and all countries produce men of genius. But it may be worth while noting that the America of his time gave room to his genius. He could rise by his own merits and industry; he did not have to lean on the patronage and favor of the great. He was a native product; American as tobacco or Indian corn. And he became one of the great citizens of the world.

Now, a man nearing seventy, a man of vast experience in men and affairs, Franklin, the wise and farseeing, looked ahead and saw trouble brewing. He thought that, somehow, the colonies should get together—divided, they were weak; united, they could be strong. He wanted a better and more reasonable relation between the colonies and England. But, though he laid a groundwork for the first and strove for the second, he could not bring about what he wanted. There was to be an explosion first—the explosion called the American Revolution.

REVOLUTION

Looking back at the American Revolution now, it seems at once inevitable and by no means inevitable.

The causes of grievance were real. And yet, with tact, patience and forethought, those causes could have been remedied. But, whether that would have been enough, no man can say.

The real differences went deeper. In the hundred and seventy years since Jamestown, the colonies had grown up. They were young men, ready to start out in the world for themselves. If they were to remain as partners in the English system, they wanted the share and responsibilities of partners.

But, to the English government, they were not young men and not potential partners. They were boys, not yet out of school, not yet ready for share or partnership. Nor was this just an English idea. It was a world idea, at the time. Colonies existed, on the whole, for the benefit of the mother country. And all laws and regulations for the benefit of the mother country should be enforced.

The English Parliament could make laws to regulate the colonies, but the colonies had no representatives in the English Parliament. The English Parliament could tax the colonies, and the colonists would have to pay those taxes or rebel.

Nevertheless, the colonies, admittedly, had certain rights of self-government. But how far did those rights extend?

Nobody quite knew. The colonists thought one thing, the English government another.

Added to these were the factors of space and time. Three million people, on one side of an ocean, had, as court of last resort and final authority, a parliament, ministers, and a king on the other side of an ocean. There was no telegraph, no telephone, no airplane, no steamship linking them together. By the time that something happened in America and the news got to England, six weeks might have passed. By the time that parliament discussed the question, reached a decision, and the news of the decision got to America, anywhere from three to six months might have passed. The king of England had never visited the colonies. Few, if any, of his ministers had ever been in the colonies. Few members of Parliament had ever been in the colonies. They were legislating for and passing final judgments upon a country they had ceased to know much about.

That wasn't their fault—things had grown that way, that was all. But it was one of the reasons why not only the American colonies ·but the South American republics eventually asserted their own independence. They were tired of being governed from the other side of an ocean. Men who were no longer, in essence, English, Spanish, Portuguese— men who had become Virginians, Brazilians, Connecticuters, Venezuelans—were tired of the whole cumbrous apparatus of distant government. They wanted more say in their own affairs.

To watch those early years just before the colonies declared their independence is like watching a field being plowed or a sea with a storm rising; like watching a woman in her labor pains or a child as it grows into manhood.

Something was going to be born—but what? Something was going to happen, explode, break, alter—but what? Not the wisest knew. But there was a ferment, a stirring, a pushing out of thought in the minds of men.

"I am a man, an American—but what does that mean? I am free, I think myself free—but what does freedom mean? I have rights as I know—but what are they—how far do they go? Is there another way than the way I have always known? Must I put up with things I don't like because they have always been that way—if not, what should I do about them?" So many Americans must have thought and wondered.

This ferment had been going on since the end of the Seven Years' War in 1763. In that war, England had broken the power of France in North America, acquired vast new dominions—and would have to pay the bill for keeping those dominions up. The English government felt, with considerable justice, that the American colonies, which benefited by the results of the war, should pay some of the bill.

The American colonists felt differently. They too had raised troops, spent money, incurred debts. They had done so willingly enough. But they didn't want to pay new taxes for the support of an imperial system in which they were not even partners.

Neither side was entirely wrong or right. It was obvious to the most clearheaded on both sides, including Franklin, that some new scheme of relations between mother country and colonies must be worked out, if the system was to go on. And such a system was worked out, much later on, in the British Commonwealth of Nations. But that was still far in the future, and the situation in 1763 was complicated by an industrious but stubborn king, George III, who chose un-intelligent and amateurish advisers.

The first warning of the Revolution came with the Stamp Act. The English government, wanting to raise money from the colonies, made a law that revenue stamps, costing from a halfpenny to eighty shillings, were to be put on all news-papers, pamphlets, licenses, commercial bills, leases, legal documents, etc., in the colonies. If you didn't buy stamps and put them on these papers, you were breaking the law.

This seemed reasonable enough to Parliament and the king's ministers—especially since it was provided that all money raised by these stamps was to be spent for "defending, protecting and securing the colonies." But it was a match dropped into a keg of powder.

Americans did not see the Stamp Act as a necessary and normal measure of government. They saw it as an extraordinary and ominous beginning of tyranny, forced upon them from outside and without their consent.

They burned stamps, they forced the agents who sold stamps to give up their jobs. They met, they protested, they got up on their hind feet and yelled. They sent remonstrances and petitions to the king. They said: "We owe you allegiance, but we have the same rights as Englishmen. It is the right of Englishmen that no taxes be imposed upon them but with their own consent, given personally or by their representatives. And we have not given that consent."

The Stamp Act was repealed and the colonies rejoiced. And yet the repeal settled nothing. It settled nothing, because men had begun to talk about Liberty in a new way. They had begun to say:

"We should stand upon the broad common ground of

natural rights . . . There ought to be no New England man, no New Yorker, known on the continent, but all of us Americans."—Christopher Gadsden of South Carolina.

"Let us consider ourselves as men—freemen—Christian freemen—separated from the rest of the world and firmly bound together by the same rights, interests and dangers . . . What have these colonies to ask, while they continue free?"— John Dickinson of Pennsylvania.

"Is life so dear, or peace so sweet, as to be purchased at the price of chains and slavery? Forbid it, Almighty God! I know not what course others may take, but as for me, give me liberty, or give me death!"—Patrick Henry of Virginia.

Liberty! It's a strong word—it gets into men's blood. It's only a puff of wind in the air at first—and then it's a rising gale. It blew through the crooked streets of Boston and the farmlands of Pennsylvania and the rolling Virginia hills. "Liberty! We'll stand up for Liberty!" It drifts in and out of the cabins of the frontier and the riflemen nod and say: "You don't have to tell us about liberty. We have it. We aim to keep it." It is tapped out on a drum where men march and drill in secret: "Come all ye sons of Liberty, unite like freeborn men . . ." It's a tide rising and a wind blowing and a drum tapping—tapping out the years that are past and the years to come.

But, three thousand miles away, in England, the industrious, stubborn king and his changing ministers hear neither the drum nor the gale. They are puzzled, disturbed, somewhat angry. These colonial children mustn't have things all their own way. Authority must be maintained. A firm hand must be shown. If Boston makes trouble, send troops to Boston. Revive an old law of Henry VIII and bring the trouble-

33

makers to England for trial. Show a firm hand. Pay no heed to the passionate protests of such great Englishmen as Burke and Pitt. "America must fear you before she can love you," says Lord North, prime minister of England. And, as for the taxing business—well, there we'll be generous. We'll repeal other duties and just put a tax on tea—a token tax. The Americans will actually get their tea cheaper than they did before. But they'll pay a tax on it—and that will show we *can* tax them—

They thought they were dealing with children. They were dealing with men. And, as was to happen many times in American history, an overseas government went wrong on the American character. They thought money was all that Americans cared about.

So the tax was put on the tea and the tea shipped over. And when the tea reached Boston, the men of Boston took it —and dumped it into Boston harbor.

That was the Boston Tea Party—December 16, 1773. And, as the tea floated away in the gray waters, so floated away all chance of a peaceful settlement.

The English government felt it could not back down. The American colonists knew they would not back down.

The English government closed the port of Boston, annulled the charter of Massachusetts, and passed other coercive acts. The colonies replied by summoning a Continental Congress. It met in Philadelphia in September, 1774—forty-five sober men from every colony but North Carolina and Georgia—as a hundred and fifty-five years before, the burgesses had met at Jamestown, as in 1620 the signers of the Mayflower Compact had met aboard the *Mayflower*. This was for a nation, now, but the same strong impulse showed itself. In crisis, unite. Get together, talk together—decide on your rights and speak them. Stand up for your rights like men. It had come a long way, that voice of rights and freedom—all the way from the marsh at Runnymede and the signing of Magna Charta. It was to go on.

On the 19th of April, 1775—a misty, farming morning—on the 19th of April and on the village green of a small farm town called Lexington, in Massachusetts, British regulars, sent from Boston to confiscate munitions, saw a line of armed farmers barring their way—American Minute Men. The British captain called on them to disperse.

"Disperse, you rebels—why don't you disperse?" he said.

"Stand your ground, men—don't fire unless fired upon—but, if they want a war, let it begin here," said the American captain. Then the shots came. And the Revolution began.

The English government had made a second mistake. It had thought that Americans would not fight. Other governments, in time to come, were to think that, too—and as mistakenly.

The British expedition got back to its base in Boston—but 273 British regulars lay dead or wounded. The colonists swarmed from their houses like angry bees and shot down the red-coated men from behind stone walls. And, two months later, on June 17, 1775, three thousand veteran British soldiers tried to take an American position, on Breed's Hill and Bunker Hill just outside Boston. They took the hill, in three tries, by direct assault—but their loss in killed and wounded was over a thousand men. Untrained but hard-shooting farmers and mechanics, commanded by amateur generals, had stood up to the best-trained infantry of their time.

They weren't to do so always. They were to suffer defeat, disaster and rout. They were to starve and run and hide. But they had developed their own technique of fighting. And they were to be led by George Washington, a man who would not give in.

One year later, June 7, 1776, Richard Henry Lee of Virginia rose in the Continental Congress and moved "That these United Colonies are and of right ought to be Free and Independent States." After nearly a month's debate, the motion was adopted, and, on July 4, 1776, the Declaration of Independence announced the birth of a new nation.

The Declaration of Independence is one of the two great cornerstones of American faith and the American way of life. Every American child has studied it at school, heard it read on national holidays, had the words sink into his mind. We take what it says as a rule that we want to live by— a goal that we strive for as a nation.

So, what does it say about men and governments—about the way in which human beings should live together, if they can?

It gives various specific reasons why the colonies wished to separate from England. But the heart and core of its doctrine are in the second paragraph. That paragraph reads:

"We hold these truths to be self-evident: that all men are created equal; that they are endowed by their Creator with certain unalienable rights; that among these are life, liberty, and the pursuit of happiness; that, to secure these rights, governments are instituted among men, deriving their just powers from the consent of the governed; that whenever any form of government becomes destructive of these ends, it is the right of the people to alter or to abolish it, and to institute new government, laying its foundation on such principles, and organizing its powers in such form, as to them shall seem most likely to effect their safety and happiness. Prudence, indeed, will dictate that governments long established should not be changed for light and transient causes; and, accordingly, all experience hath shown that mankind are more disposed to suffer, while evils are sufferable, than to right themselves by abolishing the forms to which they are accustomed. But when a long train of abuses and usurpations, pursuing invariably the same object, evidence a design to reduce them under absolute despotism, it is their right, it is their duty, to throw off such government and to provide new guards for their future security. . . ."

That was a challenge to all men—not just to three million colonists. Read it over—it is still a challenge and a summons to all men who seek for freedom.

And in that lies the importance of the Declaration. Not that the colonists met and said "We want to be independent," but that, doing so, they set down certain principles and beliefs—that all men are created equal, that all men have certain rights, that governments are made to secure these rights and derive their powers from the consent of the governed and not from the will of a king or a dictator or the special interests of a special class, that it is the right of the people to overthrow tyrants and despots and seek their own best means of governing themselves.

These ideas were not brand-new. They had been in the minds of wise men for many years—in the minds of such Englishmen as Harrington and Locke and Sidney—in the minds of a new generation then growing up in France. But here, for the first time, they were stated in short and simple words as a fighting faith for three million people at war. They were not stated as beautiful dreams for some future world but as self-evident truths. They were written down by a great and thoughtful man, Thomas Jefferson of Virginia—but they had been hammered out on the anvil of a hundred and seventy years' very practical experience of liberty and self-government on the part of most Americans. Jefferson himself had sat in the Virginia House of Burgesses—he had seen men govern themselves. He was not talking emptily—his faith had its roots in experience. And so his words march on. We have failed them often enough, as human beings do. But we believe today, as we did in 1776, that they are the right words for free men. And we mean to maintain them, even at great cost.

The Declaration was bold—a bell and a trumpet of liberty. But it did not end the Revolution. The War for Independence was a long one, a hard one, a bitter one. Counting from the battle of Lexington, it lasted for seven years.

It was a civil war as well as a national one. Many Americans—and from deep conviction—took the British side. They suffered and endured for their cause as truly as men have ever suffered and endured—and when the war was over, or before its end, many left or were driven from the colonies to start life over again in Canada, in England, in the other British possessions. And their descendants grew into the new life and made stalwart citizens of the British commonwealth.

It was an English conflict as well as an American one. Many of the best and wisest Englishmen—from Pitt to Charles James Fox—were to stand up and speak for the American cause, not because they loved England the less but because they loved liberty.

It was a war of freedom and the free-minded. From France, Lafayette, Rochambeau, and many others came to help the Americans. From the German states came von Steuben and De Kalb. From Poland, Kosciusko, and Pulaski came. It was a war of convictions. Certain families of wealth and prominence, the Jays, the Livingstons, the Lees, adopted the patriot cause. Others pledged their loyalty to England. At the start of the Revolution, George Washington was a prosperous planter, as prosperity went in those days, chiefly interested in developing and improving his farms. He had served as a soldier and surveyor on the frontier, but his tastes were peaceful and the temper of his mind, on the whole, conservative. He liked to live like a gentleman—an honorable and upright gentleman, but a gentleman used to good clothes, polite manners, pleasant company, a game of cards with friends, and a hard day in the hunting field. He liked to keep careful and accurate records of the crops he raised and the dogs he bred and the money his crops brought in—or didn't bring in. But he served seven years, without pay, as commander of the Continental Army and was the prop and mainstay of a struggling people. He was plagued by toothache, disaster, and envious enemies—he was vilified, libeled, and lampooned—he was hunted like a fox across the Jerseys—he shared the cold and the hunger of his ragged troops—and he never gave in. He had everything to lose by being a patriot—but he never gave in. He could not be bought, he could not be intimidated or exhausted—he could not be turned or diverted from the cause of liberty. And as it was with him, so was it with Paul Revere, the silversmith, print seller, engraver, Jack-of-all-trades, whose father, Apollos Revoire had come from the Isle of Jersey—and Alexander Hamilton, the brilliant youngster born in the West Indies—and John Adams, the Boston lawyer—and Samuel Adams, the radical orator of the Boston people. They believed that men should be free—and they staked their all on that conviction.

It was a curious war. Individual British commanders might be ruthless but the British high command in America, though they wished to win, did not try to crush and exterminate the American people as such. The records of Gage, the Howes, Burgoyne, Cornwallis are not black records. They fought as honorable soldiers. They had no strategy of terror. And there were no mass executions on either side.

A curious war, indeed—for it was not popular with the mass of the English people. A number of distinguished officers—Lord Jeffrey Amherst among them—declined to serve against the colonies, and recruiting lagged. So the English ministry brought over Hessians—simple peasants sold by the Prince of Hesse-Cassel at so much a head to go over and die in America for a cause they knew nothing about. And, as they were foreigners and mercenaries, the Americans hated them. And yet, after the war was done, some ten thousand of these Hessians remained in America, married, settled down, got land of their own. They were free in America, they would not be free in Hesse-Cassel. And America took them in, and they made good citizens.

It was a war for a cause, a war that went to the trumpet blast of Tom Paine, the corsetmaker turned pamphleteer who wrote: "though the flame of liberty may sometimes cease to shine, the coal can never expire." And a war fought, too, by many men not quite sure of all the issues, as all wars are.

A war fought, on the American side, by farmers, mechanics, tradesmen, fishermen, barbers, hunters, blacksmiths turned generals like Greene, huntsmen turned generals like Morgan, farmers turned generals like Washington. A war quietly endured by quiet people who saw their houses burned and their crops ravaged and cursed whoever did it and yet resolved to stay in the land. A war hailed and decried in Europe—watched by Europe—having its effects in Europe and in the minds of men who read the newspapers or heard another man talking and heard the name "Washington," the name "America," the words "common sense." The words "All men are created equal."

And at last, with the aid of France and the French fleet, it ended. Cornwallis surrendered at Yorktown, Virginia, on October 19, 1781. The preliminary treaty of peace was signed on November 30, 1782, the final treaty September 3, 1783. Ordinary men and women, poor and rich, frontiersmen, merchants and farmers, had got up on their feet and, after seven years' fighting, made a nation.

CONSTITUTION

But what sort of nation was it? The eyes of Europe looked and wondered. It was weak, it was new. It was an experiment, an oddity, a hope, a wish, an idea—but hardly a nation.

Some of its most fertile fields had been devastated by war. Many of its most substantial men had left or been driven out.

Hardly born as a nation, it staggered under a load of debt. Its money had depreciated to a point where "not worth a continental" was a byword. Its trade had been badly hit. Its industries, hampered by war, were almost at a standstill. Its credit was nil.

Worse than that, it was not one state but thirteen states which had fought side by side but without entire agreement.

Its government was a clumsy debating society—the Continental Congress. Its army, even in victory, was still unpaid.

Surely, it must fall apart in a few years—fall apart into thirteen little quarreling nations—fall into the hand of some stronger foreign power—or fall into bloody civil revolution and anarchy.

Or, if none of these things happened—well, it would certainly need a king, a dictator, an emperor, a man with a strong hand. Perhaps one of the minor European royalties might be persuaded to take on the troublesome job. Or perhaps the Americans would set up an imitation despot of their own.

And yet, it was a hope, a wish, a dream—something men with all sorts of different names had fought for and died for. Had they fought and died in vain?

They wondered—these who had seen it and those who had merely heard of it—Lafayette and Fox and Burgoyne, the king of Prussia, the king of France, the king of England.

And, as they wondered, the nation made itself.

THE PILLARS OF THE HOUSE

There is a time, after every revolution, when men have to sit down, take stock, and decide on what sort of government they mean to live under. Such a time came to America when the delegates to the Constitutional Convention met in Philadelphia, May 25, 1787.

There were fifty-five of them, nine of whom were foreign-born. That is not very many men to decide on the future of a nation. But they included Washington, Franklin, Madison, Hamilton, Randolph, Mason, Dickinson—the brains of the American states, with the exception of Jefferson, then in France on a diplomatic mission.

The average age of the Convention was forty-two. They were neither old men nor striplings. They were men tried by war and revolution, men with practical experience who wanted to set up a workable system under which their children could breathe free air.

They argued and debated many points. The small states were jealous of the large ones. The propertied men wanted to safeguard their property. The debtors wanted easy money. The firm States' Rights men wanted a confederation rather than a federation. But in the end, they worked out the Constitution.

The first purpose of the Constitution, as stated was, "to form a more perfect Union." How did they go about it?

They devised this system of government: a Congress, made up of two houses, a House of Representatives and a Senate—a President—a Supreme Court.

The Congress was to pass laws for the general welfare of the people. The President to execute and administer these laws. The Supreme Court was to pass on certain debatable cases of law.

The Congress was to meet once a year, to debate and pass laws. The President could not convoke it (except upon extraordinary occasions), adjourn it, or abolish it. It had to meet, whether he wanted it to meet or not.

All power comes from the people, and the Congress was given wide powers. They are listed in the Constitution. They include the powers to declare war, raise and support armies, levy taxes, regulate commerce, borrow money, etc., etc.

All power comes from the people—but there were thirteen

states concerned. So the two houses of Congress were to be set up in different ways.

The representatives of the House of Representatives were to serve for a term of two years and they were to be selected on a basis of population, that is to say, the bigger states would have more representatives than the smaller ones—and the House of Representatives initiated all money bills.

But, to take care of the rights of the small states, each state, no matter how big or small it was, was to have two senators in the Senate. They served for a six-year term. And a bill had to pass both House and Senate before it was submitted to the President.

The President, elected for four years, had wide powers, too. He was Commander in Chief of the Army and Navy. He was to administer and execute the laws. If he didn't like a bill passed by Congress, he could veto it. But, after that, if a two-thirds majority of both Houses voted for the bill, it would become a law in spite of his veto.

He had power to make treaties, but only if a two-thirds majority of the Senate concurred. He had power to appoint ambassadors, judges of the Supreme Court, and other administrative officers—but, with the advice and consent of the Senate.

In the Supreme Court was vested the judicial power of the United States. The justices of the Supreme Court were appointed "during good behaviour"—no fixed term. Whether or not the Founders of the Republic intended the Supreme Court to be a final court of review over acts of Congress is an arguable point. But that power has been so assumed and so admitted. If the Supreme Court declares an act of Congress "unconstitutional," that act goes out the window. At a future time, of course, a later Supreme Court may decide, as it has done on occasion, that a similar act or law is constitutional after all. It is quite free to do so. In practice, the Supreme Court acts as a guardian of the law, and a brake upon hasty legislation. No Supreme Court yet known to the United States, for instance, could affirm a law persecuting Jews as Jews—for such a law, even if passed by Congress and signed by the President, would directly violate the first amendment to the Constitution.

All this sounds like a rather complicated system. But it is both a flexible and a workable system. It has been well called a "system of checks and balances." No one branch of the government has complete and despotic power. All three branches of the government—legislative, executive, judicial—take part in running the affairs of the nation.

The Founders recognized that all power comes from the people. They therefore set up a Congress made up (in both houses, now) of delegates representing the people. But, lest the large and populous states should oppress the smaller ones, they gave each state two votes in the Senate and gave senators three times as long a term as representatives. The senators, supposedly, were to be somewhat older men, serving a longer term, and acting as a check and a balance to both House and President.

They wanted a strong head of the state, because most of them had had experience of a nation run entirely by a Congress. And they knew that you could not run a nation by committee. So they gave the President broad powers—powers so broad that, in time of war particularly, he is one of the strongest executives in the world. But, as they did not wish him to become a despot, they provided for a presidential election every four years—they provided that Congress could pass bills over his veto—they made other provisions limiting his powers.

They provided, in the Supreme Court, for a supreme judicial authority.

And they provided—and this is very important—that the Constitution could be amended. It was not a fixed and unalterable document. In times to come, changes in it could be made. And it has been so amended twenty-one times—though the process of amendment is both difficult and lengthy.

Some things they did not provide for. They did not provide specifically for a Cabinet—for a secretary of state, a secretary of war, and so forth, though they admitted that there would be "executive departments" and heads of "executive departments." They did not provide for political parties or a party system. They provided for an Electoral College to elect the President—and that did not work out in practice. Technically, the President is still elected by the Electoral College—but, in practice, these electors are on a party ticket and vote for their party candidate for president. But most of the things they provided have stood the test of time. There are defects in the system. But it works.

Then the Constitution had to be ratified, of course, by at least nine of the thirteen states, and after much discussion was so ratified.

But even then, men were not content.

A government had been established. But what were the rights of the average citizen under that government?

The first Congress of the United States, meeting in New York in the autumn of 1789, passed ten amendments to the original Constitution. Known as the "Bill of Rights," they are as follows:

Article I

Congress shall make no law respecting an establishment of religion, or prohibiting the free exercise thereof; or abridging the freedom of speech or of the press; or the right of the people peaceably to assemble, and to petition the government for a redress of grievances.

Article II

A well-regulated militia being necessary to the security of a free State, the right of the people to keep and bear arms shall not be infringed.

Article III

No soldier shall, in time of peace, be quartered in any house, without the consent of the owner, nor in time of war but in a manner to be prescribed by law.

Article IV

The right of the people to be secure in their persons, houses, papers, and effects, against unreasonable searches and seizures, shall not be violated; and no warrants shall issue but upon probable cause, supported by oath or affirmation, and particularly describing the place to be searched, and the person or things to be seized.

Article V

No person shall be held to answer for a capital or otherwise infamous crime, unless on a presentment or indictment of a grand jury, except in cases arising in the land or naval forces, or in the militia, when in actual service in time of war or public danger; nor shall any person be subject for the same offence to be twice put in jeopardy of life or limb; nor shall be compelled in any criminal case to be a witness against himself, nor be deprived of life, liberty, or property, without due process of law; nor shall private property be taken for public use without just compensation.

Article VI

In all criminal prosecutions, the accused shall enjoy the right to a speedy and public trial, by an impartial jury of the State and district wherein the crime shall have been committed, which district shall have been previously ascertained by law; and to be informed of the nature and cause of the accusation; to be confronted with the witnesses against him; to have compulsory process for obtaining witnesses in his favor, and to have the assistance of counsel for his defence.

Article VII

In suits at common law, where the value of controversy shall exceed twenty dollars, the right of trial by jury shall be preserved, and no fact tried by a jury shall be otherwise re-examined in any court of the United States, than according to the rules of the common law.

Article VIII

Excessive bail shall not be required, nor excessive fines imposed, nor cruel and unusual punishments inflicted.

Article IX

The enumeration in the Constitution of certain rights shall not be construed to deny or disparage others retained by the people.

Article X

The powers not delegated to the United States by the Constitution, nor prohibited by it to the States, are reserved to the States respectively, or to the people.

And again men had stepped ahead. The Constitution and the Bill of Rights are the second and third cornerstones of the American faith. Freedom of speech, freedom of worship, freedom from persecution, right of trial by jury, were guaranteed to Americans. Men, created equal, born with inalienable rights, were now free to work out their own destiny.

THE YOUNG REPUBLIC

With the peaceful inauguration of George Washington as the first President of the United States, the American Revolution ended.

It had been a real revolution—a long and difficult travail, full of hardship, struggle, bitterness, and the overturning of old habits and customs. But it did not eat its children and it had no aftermath of vengeance. The Hessians who stayed in the country were not hunted down and annihilated. Some loyalists who returned were harshly treated—others came back and settled down peacefully as citizens of the new state. There was neither blood bath nor purge. There was bitter political dispute—but no small group of men plotted in secret to overthrow the government by force of arms. There were a couple of minor and local revolts, based on genuine grievances—Shays' Rebellion in 1786—the Whisky Rebellion in 1794. Both collapsed when the government showed itself able to put down rebellion—and nobody was hanged for either of them. Shays and his temporary rebels received a general amnesty—the leaders of the Whisky Rebellion were convicted of treason and then pardoned by the President.

Why was this? Certainly not because Americans were more virtuous than anybody else. Americans never have been more virtuous than other people. They were lucky, that is all —lucky in working out a system that allowed for different points of view—lucky in the men who first guided the young republic.

These were human men. They had faults. They made mistakes. But not one of them wanted or planned to be a despot. Not one of them felt that the only way to rule was to kill or imprison people who didn't agree with him.

They had a dream before them—the dream of a free republic. And they tried, quite consciously, to live up to that dream. At times it was a little stilted, at others a little funny. They thought of themselves as early Romans—the Romans of the Roman Republic they had read about in Plutarch. A small-town lawyer who wrote a letter to the newspaper was quite apt to sign it "Cincinnatus" or "Brutus Jr." And there is an unhappy statue of George Washington in a toga. All that is easy to laugh at—and visitors often laughed. But when these men spoke of "Republican virtue" and "Republican simplicity" they meant something by it. They tried to live up to those words—to the dream of a free republic, even finer than that of the early days of Rome.

Let us take a few of these men and see what they did and thought.

George Washington first, for not only the success of the Revolution but the successful founding of the Republic hinged, to a great degree, on the character of this man.

If you look at Washington from one point of view, you will find him strict, cool, dignified, rather unapproachable. Not a man who liked the smell and sweat of the crowd—not a man who mixed very easily with men who were not his social equals. A strong man, strong in body and strong in mind, but a mind with no particular inventive or philosophic turn to it. A hot temper, usually under control, sometimes flaring into bursts of wrath. A man of no great, crowd-winning phrases. And yet—

He never flinched at any time from any burden that was laid upon him. He could have had any reward from the nation he founded—but when the head of a foolish little coterie wrote to him and suggested that he be king of the new nation, he did not merely decline the suggestion, he said in the plainest and sharpest of words: "If you have any regard for yourself or posterity or respect for me, banish these thoughts from your mind and never communicate as from yourself or anyone else, a sentiment of the like nature." A man who loved his home, he did not see it for six years during the Revolution. A rich man and a careful manager, he pledged himself and his fortune to the cause of freedom and saw his riches dwindle without a word. His ambition was for his country and for his countrymen. He was human and often despaired of their sense, their patriotism, and everything about them—but he never stopped working for them till the day he died. And so, even when they abused him—and that happened, too—his countrymen trusted George Washington. He was a great, stable fact—a fact of character. No matter at what cost, he would do what he thought was right. They had no small affectionate nicknames for him—he was not that sort of man. But when men called him "the father of his country," it was not an eloquent phrase but the bare and simple truth.

Washington was the first President of the United States, John Adams the second. Short, cocky, critical, independent, caustic, a lawyer, the son of a farmer, the great-grandson of an out-of-work carpenter who had emigrated from England in 1636, John Adams spoke his mind wherever he was. He was able, prickly, tart—and capable of great and unselfish devotion to his country. A New Englander, he worked and strove to make Washington, the Virginian, commander in chief of the Continental Army, because he thought Washington was the best man for the job. A revolutionary with no taste for blood, he found the Boston Tea Party, "the most magnificent movement of all." A man of stiff principles, he quarreled with Thomas Jefferson on principle, wrote bitter and venomous things about Jefferson in his diary—and made up his quarrel in old age with such grace and mellowness that the final correspondence between the two men has the amplitude and ranging thought of old but unwearied gods discussing the small but vital affairs of men. A lawyer who had never been a seaman, he founded the American Navy. An unpopular president, he did his duty as president with stubborn devotion. He lacked the easy gifts that would have made men love him, instead of regarding him with respectful irritation. But he was one of the first political philosophers of America—and his caustic, questioning, and stubborn spirit still survives in the New England mind.

Thomas Jefferson, the third President, a Virginian, was one of those universal men whom it is hard to compress in a few words. Tall, rawboned, gray-eyed, sandy-haired, he was an inventor, a thinker, a writer, a philosopher, a practical politician, and a man who believed continuously in the worth and virtue of the people. He designed a new and efficient plow, and wrote the Declaration of Independence. He was a notable architect and his own house, Monticello, built to his own plans, is one of the beautiful houses of the world. He was always interested in the new, the future thing—what men could be if they chose, what men could be if they willed. He loved the arts, played the violin, had an eye for form and composition. He could be as bitter and as unfair as Adams in his private and temporary judgment of his contemporaries— he could be circuitous in his politics and disingenuous in some of his dealings. But he was the first great democrat of America —and his faith in the people never wavered through his long life. "Only lay down true principles and adhere to them inflexibly," he wrote in 1816, after a vast experience of men and government. "Do not be frightened into their surrender by the alarms of the timid or the croakings of the wealthy against the ascendancy of the people. . . . The true foundations of republican government is the equal right of every citizen, in his person and property, and in their management . . . I know that laws and institutions must go hand in hand with the progress of the human mind. As that becomes more developed, more enlightened, as new discoveries are made, new truths disclosed . . . institutions must advance also and keep pace with the times." A man of the future, he believed in equal and exact justice to all men and said of himself, "I steer my bark with Hope ahead and Fear astern."

His grave in Virginia is the grave of a believer in man, the grave of one who had known both the best and the worst of mankind, and yet never altered his faith in what common men could do and be.

Alexander Hamilton, brilliant, fluent, attractive, a brave soldier, an able writer, a great financier, was another of the Founders. He was Washington's favorite aide-de-camp and the first Secretary of the Treasury of the United States. Where Jefferson hoped for a future America, composed largely of self-supporting and independent farmers, Hamilton's mind turned toward industry and capital. He had no particular belief in the people—he thought they should be guided and ruled by men more intelligent than they. He admitted his liking for "the rich, the well-born and the well-bred." He was not an equalitarian, except on the score of intelligence—he did not believe in the murmuring voice of the crowd. Yet it would be a great mistake to think of Hamilton as anything but the revolutionary which he was. He wanted a strong centralized state, run by the best and ablest people perhaps under a monarchy—but he wanted a free and independent state which would be a model for the world. Loving splendor, he cared little for money, and none of it stuck to his fingers. He and Jefferson were born to be adversaries, for they cherished different ideas on the nature of man. But the actual adoption of the Constitution which made the United States possible owes as much to Hamilton as it does to any one man—and the restoration of the national credit is almost entirely his work. He died in an unnecessary duel, on a point of honor, a duel which could have been avoided by a man with less personal courage—died at forty-seven, having left his strong and personal mark on the nation.

Such were four of the men who founded the young republic—men as different as men could be and yet united in the desire to make a free nation. There were many others—Gallatin the Swiss—the Lee Brothers of Virginia—Rutledge of South Carolina—Madison and Monroe, each one to be president in turn, each one brought up on the ideas of these older men. And there were, on the frontier, yet others, for all through the Revolution the hunters and the first settlers were beginning to stream through the passes of the Allegheny Mountains. There they would be free of all laws—and yet the first thing they did was to get together and make their own laws. In Kentucky and Tennessee, the new settlers formed their own governments—and wrote them down. Hard-bitten frontiersmen, veterans of Indian warfare, laid aside their rifles for an hour and met together. They weren't quite sure whom they wanted to belong to, but they knew they meant to live free. The Revolution itself might be a far rumor to them—but they had bought their lands at the price of blood, and they meant to hold them in freedom. Things were practical, on the frontier, and freedom was not only practical but a necessity.

And so, after some five presidents had been peaceably elected, a second and rather inconclusive war with England fought in 1812, it began to be admitted, by competent observers, that this new hope, this new experiment, this new republic of the New World stood some chance of surviving its birth-pains. But how did it fit into the affairs of the world?

It was still a city of refuge and a symbol of hope for anyone from Britain or the Continent who wanted to try his fortune there. And some came, and were most bitterly disappointed at not finding a ready-made Eden. And some came and were cheated and fooled and called its ideals a sham. And some came and throve.

But, as a country, as a nation, it was neither a great nor an important power. It had shown a few queer and interesting manifestations. Under Jefferson's presidency, for instance, the United States had refused to pay tribute to the Barbary pirates, and the American Navy, operating four thousand miles from its base, had forced respect for the Stars and Stripes on bold and enterprising corsairs. Under Jefferson's presidency, also, the vast lands of Louisiana had been bought from France. In the war of 1812, while Washington had been captured by the British and the White House burned, a general called Andrew Jackson had won a considerable victory over British regulars at New Orleans, and American privateers and fir-built frigates had stood up well against the greatest navy in the world. However, in the eyes of Europe—and rightly enough—these were relatively small and unimportant matters. The United States had no trained and disciplined army—no Grand Fleet. It remained a question mark—somewhere off on one side of the map. It was there—but it played but small part in the affairs of the world.

To the Americans, however, the situation was somewhat different. They were wholly contented to have things just that way. They did not want a big army or a vast navy. They did not want to engage in European quarrels. They wanted to push ahead and develop their own land. As far as the other nations of the world were concerned, they wanted to trade with them, exchange ideas and goods, maintain peaceable relations. But that was all.

And, not only did they want to do this, they could do it. The east and west coasts of the North American continent were protected by two vast oceans. The nations to the north and south of the United States were not strongly militarized nations. The United States could work out its own way of life, without constant threat of aggression from some other power. And it did so for many years.

Only one possibility remained—further colonization of the Western Hemisphere by some strong outside power and the building up, in either North or South America of a state, strongly tied to Europe, which might be hostile to the United States. So, in 1823, after the former colonies of Spain in the New World had thrown off the rule of Spain and set up their own republics, the then President of the United States, James Monroe, made the following statement of American policy:

"The occasion has been judged proper for asserting, as a principle . . . that the American continents, by the free and independent condition which they have assumed and maintained are henceforth not to be considered as subjects for future colonization by any European power."

As regards intervention in the affairs of North or South America by any outside powers, Monroe had this to say:

"The citizens of the United States cherish sentiments the most friendly in favor of the liberty and happiness of their fellow-men on that side of the Atlantic. In the wars of the European powers in matters relating to themselves we have never taken any part, nor does it comport with our policy so to do. It is only when our rights are invaded or seriously menaced that we resent injuries or make preparation for our defence . . . With the movements in this hemisphere we are, of necessity, more immediately connected, and by causes which must be obvious . . . The political system of the allied powers is essentially different in this respect from that of America. This difference proceeds from that which exists in their respective governments. And to the defence of our own, which has been achieved by the loss of so much blood and treasure . . . this whole nation is devoted. We owe it, therefore, to candor, and to the amicable relations existing between the United States and those powers, to declare that we should consider any attempt on their part to extend their system to any portion of this hemisphere as dangerous to our peace and safety. With the existing colonies or dependencies of any European power, we have not interfered and shall not interfere. But with the governments who have declared their independence and maintained it, and whose independence we have . . . acknowledged, we could not view any interposition for the purpose of oppressing them, or controlling in any other manner their destiny, by any European power, in any other light than as the manifestation of an unfriendly disposition towards the United States."

That was the Monroe Doctrine. It is still a cardinal point of American policy.

It sprang from necessity and it followed conversations between England and the United States on these new developments in the New World. Stripped of diplomatic language, it said: "No meddling or interference with the affairs of the New World by outside powers! We, the United States, will fight, if that is done." And it went unchallenged by the world's great powers.

Why?

At that time, all Europe was still recovering from the shock and aftermath of the Napoleonic Wars. The first great impulse of westward colonization on the part of France and Spain had spent itself. Spain was not strong enough to reconquer her colonies in the Western Hemisphere, once they had made up their minds to be free. Britain, fearful of her Continental rivals and friendly to the Latin-American republics, supported the American policy. France wanted peace. Russia had already established trading posts near San Francisco, but she had no burning colonial ambitions and, after negotiation, was perfectly willing to restrict her claims on the American continent to latitude 54°40'. So the thing was done. And not only the United States, but all the other states of the Western Hemisphere were free to go their own ways.

The United States has not always dealt wisely and justly with her neighbors in the New World. But they know—and the United States knows—that any attempt at armed invasion or conquest of any state in the Western Hemisphere by any outside power would immediately result in war between the United States and that power. It could not be otherwise.

The Monroe Doctrine was a practical necessity. But behind it there was also a passionate desire—a desire that the New World should be a New World indeed, free of the feuds, the entanglements, the struggles for power of the Old World. Jefferson put this as clearly as anyone when he said: "Our first and fundamental maxim should be, never to entangle ourselves in the broils of Europe. Our second never to let Europe intermeddle with cis-Atlantic affairs . . . The events in Europe cast a gloomy cloud . . . Yet I will not believe that our labors are lost. I shall not die without a hope that light and liberty are on steady advance . . . And even should the cloud of barbarism and despotism again obscure the science and liberties of Europe, this country remains to preserve and restore light and liberty to them . . ."

That is plain speech and Americans for many years were

to feel just like that. They were making something new and they knew it—an experiment in life and government and the rights of man. They wanted to be let alone to make that experiment. Rightly or wrongly, they felt themselves to be a dedicated people. Any Europeans who wanted to come over and help them in their experiment were welcome, but they would have to drop their old loyalties at the front door. They would have to say out loud that the American way of life was the right way of life—and any criticism of that way of life was hotly resented.

That attitude had in it the seeds of both good and evil. It made Americans self-reliant, independent, stubbornly conscious of their own liberties, and always willing to take a chance on the present for the sake of the future. It gave them a reputation for boastfulness, bragging, and thin-skinned resentment of criticism. When an American showed a European a few log cabins set in a malarious swamp and called the result a great city, the European didn't know whether to laugh in his guide's face or to make the soothing remarks that one makes to the insane. But the American was not seeing what was in front of his eyes—the sharp-nosed pigs in the street, the agued and sallow people. He was seeing what ought to be there in fifty years' time—and he was perfectly willing to call the place New Athens or Palmyra or Eden, and find nothing absurd in the name. And, if the European pointed out that the girls' seminary in West Magalopolis was hardly yet the equal of Oxford as a center of learning—or that the half-grown city of Washington contained nothing as beautiful as the Parthenon—why, then, the American considered the European a stuck-up and prejudiced fellow who couldn't appreciate the blessings of liberty when he saw them—while the European thought of the American as an ignorant and boastful child. And so, there were misunderstandings—and are today.

America had broken away from Europe, both politically and spiritually. And it is fair to say, as well, that Europe neither asked for nor wanted American co-operation in world affairs. The American ambassador or minister, Mr. Smith in his plain clothes, without a decoration or a title of nobility, was not an impressive figure at a European court. If he happened to be a remarkable man—as some of them were—well then, yes, he was well-received and made a good deal of. But you wouldn't ask for his advice or hope for the co-operation of his country in a matter of general European interest. There was friendliness, there was interest in the American experiment. A distinguished American, like Daniel Webster, visiting Britain and the Continent, would be gladly welcomed there. And, continually, the tide of emigration flowed to America— the tide of men and money that must build up any new country. Yet, in spite of that tide and in spite of another link—the eager if unselective way in which America still looked to the old countries for books, art, music, architecture, science, and people who knew about these things—the gradual recognition on the part of Britain and the Continent that individual Americans, too, could add to the world's knowledge—the two hemispheres slowly drifted apart, in thought and feeling and ways of life.

It was inevitable that they should.

To the average American of, say, 1840, Europe was a museum of the past. Interesting, if you wanted to go there— but a museum of the past, a symbol of everything he had tried to get away from. If he thought about Europe at all.

To the average European, of the same period, America was a half-civilized wilderness where people got scalped by Indians. Cousin John wrote queer letters back from there, but Cousin John had always had odd ideas.

And, meanwhile, the country grew.

It grew by leaps and bounds—it stretched out to the west and the south and the northwest. To use an American phrase, it grew like nothing on earth. The Thirteen States, so long penned in behind the mountain wall of the Appalachians, suddenly spread and ran and overflowed like quicksilver. By 1821, eleven more states had entered the Union—Vermont, Mississippi, Alabama, Illinois, Indiana, Kentucky, Tennessee, Louisiana, Maine, Missouri, Ohio. Men and women packed up their goods and loaded them on wagons and moved a thousand miles, with their children, their few and cherished possessions, their slips of rosebushes and apple seedlings, their Bibles, their books and their guns—to find a new home in the rich and dangerous western lands. They floated down the rivers in flatboats, they fought Indian tribes and the weather, they starved and suffered and planted themselves in the land. Single men, adventurous men, drifted out to the frontier, following some impulse that haunted their hearts like the call of the wild geese. Immigrants from Europe, Danes, Swedes, Germans, Irishmen, suddenly found themselves, after a long and trying voyage that should have been hardship enough, starting out overland to follow the sun in its course for days and days till, at last, after many days, they reached an empty prairie, and fed the beasts that had brought them there and out of logs or sod, made their first American house.

Why?

They would have said, any one of them, that they went

to better themselves. And, often, they did better themselves. Yet the lands they had left behind were fertile enough for most men.

The drive and pulse and speed of American expansion cannot be explained by any logic. It happened because it happened. The frontier—the chance of the frontier—the fertile earth waiting for men to struggle with it—was a magnet that drew the brave and the daring as it drew the misfit, the ill-adjusted, and the people who did not get on well at home. Where there had been no men before but the wandering Indian tribes, there were, suddenly, men. Men who came from all over the world. They besieged and conquered a continent nearly three thousand miles wide in the lifetime of one man. The drive had its cost in struggle, blood, and war. American settlers came to Texas early—as early as 1823. In 1835, the American settlers there broke away from the Mexican government and established the independent republic of Texas. They asked for annexation to the United States, but for ten years the question remained unsolved, and Texas maintained its own existence. Then in 1846, at the cost of war with Mexico, not only Texas but New Mexico and California, became part of the growing Republic. Many sincere and thoughtful Americans denounced the war with Mexico as a war of aggression—others supported it as a fulfillment of the American destiny. It can only be said that the Texans, once having tasted independence, had no intention of returning under Mexican rule and that the march west to the Pacific could hardly have bypassed Texas, once American settlers were firmly established there. And so, again, new, vast lands were added to the growing Union.

In fifty-one years, Americans had gone from the Atlantic

to the Pacific Ocean, settled the Middle West, explored and settled in the Northwest and the Southwest, crossed mountains as high as the Alps and rivers broader than the Danube, staggered for days over plains of alkali and the desert lands of Death Valley and brought the Stars and Stripes and the drawling American lingo to regions that had been marked down on the maps "Great American Desert. Unknown." Americans—and the Jewish peddler with his pack, and the Englishman looking for fortune, and the German, the Swiss, the Frenchman, the Italian, the Scandinavian—the veteran of Napoleon's wars and the exiles of '30 and '48 and the starving Irish peasant—every man who wanted a new chance.

And, meanwhile, there was another drive, and a great one. Under the spur of the Industrial Revolution, the making of machines that should do the work of many men, American industry and manufacture rose and hummed. Americans bought, borrowed, copied, stole, invented, improved, the designs of lathes, looms, engines, all power-driven appliances. They were used to ingenious tinkering—the New England Yankee, for instance, was famous for it—the Connecticut farmer was born a Jack-of-all-trades. They had water power, coal, iron, all the metals. They had first-class craftsmen—the sailing ships they built were the wonders of the world. They labored under no restrictions, not even wise ones—ingenuity and invention had full play. There were at least four men who invented steamboats before Fulton, who got the credit, saw his first crude steamboat chug up the waters of the Hudson. They were willing to pay for brains and skill—any sort of skilled craftsman would have a future in America. And a Yankee called Eli Whitney had already invented the cotton gin.

The cotton gin was an extremely simple and typically American invention. Before it, green seed cotton, native American cotton, had had to be cleaned of its seeds laboriously and by hand. It took a Negro a day to clean a few pounds. So native American cotton wasn't worth much as a crop—it was too hard to produce, even with slave labor.

The cotton gin, cleaning the cotton by machinery, soon changed all that. Invented in 1792, it soon spread all over the South. The production of cotton in the United States increased from 140,000 pounds in 1791 to 89,000,000 in 1810. Before that, in the South, the big cash crops had been tobacco and indigo. Now cotton was king. And the markets of the world were hungry for cotton. And cotton meant slaves and more cotton meant more slaves.

Why was this? There were several reasons. Negro slavery in the South was an old institution. It had been practiced to some extent in the North, but it had largely died out there. For one thing, the climate was harsher. For another thing, the small New England farm—or the frontier farm—was based largely on family effort. It had no one ready cash crop. Slave labor did not pay—there were too many things against it.

This was not true of the South. There the climate favored slave labor. It was warmer and milder—the Negro, just brought over from Africa, stood a better chance of survival. And from the first, there had been a crop, tobacco, which unskilled hands could cultivate on a large scale.

Nevertheless, slavery in the South seemed, at one time, a dying institution. Both Washington and Jefferson hoped to see it die out. Many of the most thoughtful men in the South hoped to see it die. Leaving out any questions of human right or human wrong, it was a wasteful and backward way of tilling the land. The slave, except from loyalty, could hardly be expected to give to his master's land the care that the free man gives to his own. The planter, on the other hand, if he was a decent man, had the responsibility of his slaves, year in and year out. He was tied, in a curious way, to the system by which he profited.

With the rise of cotton, however, the picture changed. More cotton meant more slaves and more slaves meant more cotton and both meant a chance of riches. So slavery, instead of dying out of the South, became firmly entrenched there.

Not that all Southerners were slaveholders. Far from it. A few men owned many slaves. They were a small minority. Others owned a few slaves or one slave. They were still a minority. Slavery was profitable, on the whole, for the large plantation owner—moderately profitable to the middle-sized owner—impossible for the small and struggling farmer who had no money to buy a slave. But the slaveowners, on the whole, were the rich and leading men of the community. They called the tune.

So, all the time that the great American expansion to the west was going on, two different systems of life were growing up in the settled states, side by side: the growing industry of the North, combined with a free agriculture; the farming, plantation system of the South, with its slave labor.

In time, these two systems were bound to collide, and they did collide. They were too different not to come into conflict. Abraham Lincoln put it in a nutshell when he said: " 'A house divided against itself cannot stand.' I believe this government cannot endure permanently half slave and half free. I do not expect the Union to be dissolved, I do not expect the house to fall, but I do expect it will cease to be divided. It will become all one thing, or all the other."

Through the years of the growing Republic there had been a continuous struggle for power between North and South, flaring up, dying down, flaring up again. It centered upon the new western states now coming into the Union. Were these states to be slave or free? Were they to adopt the southern system or the northern system? If one side won all the new states, the other side was bound to be outvoted, eventually, in Congress. Various compromises were made at various times. But they did not settle the issue, they only postponed the conflict. The South, which had led the Union at one time—four of the first five presidents were Virginians, saw itself being gradually forced into a position of dependence upon the North, both economically and politically. And, for the South to have to set up its own industries would have required a breaking away from the whole plantation system.

To this there were added two questions of principle.

The first was that of States' rights. Just what and how much did the Union mean? Was it a lasting, unbreakable bond between all the states or was it merely a partnership from which any state could withdraw if that state chose to do so? Which meant more, the word "United" or the word "States"? Was the United States a tree which could not be cut up and divided without killing the tree? Or was it a business arrangement that could be liquidated without damage? And—the same old question that had plagued men's minds through the years—was a man an American first and a Virginian second, or a Virginian first and an American second?

The second question of principle was that of the existence

of human slavery in a country vowed to freedom and human rights. And the two questions became inextricably mixed together.

In the North, there arose devoted and religious men and women who denounced the whole institution of slavery as an intolerable human wrong. They spoke wildly, at times, but from a burning conviction. They protested violently against every extension of slavery, they denounced all laws that allowed a southern master to recover slaves who had escaped to the North, they set up secret organizations to help slaves escape from slavery, they sent men and guns to the frontier territories to make sure that these would be free soil. They were a minority, but a convinced, obstreperous, devoted, and resolute minority. They were called abolitionists. And, in denouncing slavery, they denounced the whole South.

To those who believed in them, they were heroes of God. To the South, they were fanatic zealots, meddling in something that was none of their business. When the abolitionists wrote books on the wrongs and abuses of slavery, the southern newspapers retorted by pointing out the long hours and small pay of New England mill hands. That was true enough, but it did not settle the dispute. Gradually, and then rapidly, the two points of view hardened. Southerners who did not believe in slavery found themselves insisting that the South had a right to manage her own affairs, even if she had to leave the Union to do so. Northerners, who were not abolitionists, found themselves insisting that the Union must be preserved, even at the cost of civil war. And, after an armed raid on the Virginia town of Harpers Ferry by John Brown and his men on October 16, 1859—a raid that failed in its purpose of freeing slaves but set John Brown's harsh name imperishably on the roll of American history—the crack in the Union widened into a chasm. To the South, John Brown was a murderous fanatic who had tried to stir up the one thing most dreaded by all Southerners—a slave rebellion. To the North—even to those who denounced his actions—he was a brave man who died for his ideas like a hero. In the next presidential election—1860—the new Republican party carried every free state. The southern vote was split between three candidates, Douglas, Breckenridge, and Bell, and the Republican candidate, Abraham Lincoln of Illinois, became President of the United States.

ABRAHAM LINCOLN

Who was this Abraham Lincoln of Illinois?

He was born in a log cabin in Kentucky, February 12, 1809, the son of a rather shiftless but amiable frontiersman named Thomas Lincoln and his wife, Nancy Hanks, the illegitimate daughter of a woman who had come from Virginia to Kentucky over the Wilderness Road with her child in her arms. He was born on a bed of cornhusks and bearskins, in a cabin that had only one window and one door. And today, there is a huge marble building in Washington —the Lincoln Memorial—where crowds come every day to look at his seated statue, and they drop their voices a little when they look at it, for the face is rugged and brooding and the face of a great man. And today, the smallest coin we have —the copper penny—has his face upon it—his face and the word "Liberty." And both things are right—the great statue and the small common coin of the people—for he was a great man, and he lived and died for the common people and loved them.

The Lincolns had been in America for generations—strong people, grist-of-the-mill people, never rising very high in the world, never sinking very low. Lincoln's grandfather was a captain of Virginia militia who moved to early Kentucky after the Revolution and was killed by Indians there. Lincoln's grandmother came to Kentucky as we have said. On both sides, they were pioneer people—and Lincoln's was a pioneer boyhood.

Tom Lincoln moved to Indiana, with his wife and children—young Abraham and his sister. They cleared their ground, built their cabin, slept on beds of dry leaves. They went barefoot most of the year. The father hunted and did a little farming—the mother took care of cabin and children. When he was eight, young Abraham knew how to use an ax—when he was eight, he and his sister were walking nine miles and back a day to a one-room school.

He was nine when his mother died. His father married again—a good and thoughtful woman who took care of the children as if they had been her own. He grew up tall and strong—a fine axman, a first-class wrestler. He worked for various people, split rails for one, did chores for another. But he was always reading and thinking. There were not many books on the Indiana frontier, but he tracked them down and got hold of them, reading them again and again. He told his friends: "The things I want to know are in books; my best friend is the man who'll git me a book I ain't read." He would read late at night, stretched out before the firelight. Read, and think about what he had read.

He liked to talk and joke, and he was a wonderful story-teller. Some people said he liked telling stories better than working—but everybody admitted he could work hard when he wanted. The stories ran through his life—he was always telling them—sometimes to make a point, sometimes just because they were funny. But with the stories, there was something else—a deep melancholy that came over him like a wave. When this melancholy oppressed him, he looked like the saddest man on earth, and perhaps he was.

He wanted something—he didn't know what he wanted. He kept a store for a while and got into debt. The debts took him years to pay but he paid them all. He read law. He was a flatboatsman, a surveyor, a postmaster. He made speeches—and found out that he could make speeches, talking plain talk to people who understood plain talk. At twenty-five, he was elected to the Illinois legislature. There he learned about politics and the ways of men. But he was still looking, still seeking. He fell in love, but the girl died before they could be married—as his mother had died, as his sister had died at eighteen. Death kept coming into his life like a strain of tragic music. All the funny stories could not alter the fact of death—the curious unanswerable fact.

At twenty-eight, with seven dollars in his pocket, he came to Springfield, Illinois, to set up in business as a lawyer. Springfield, at that time, had 1,500 people in it. It was not the biggest town Lincoln had ever seen—his flatboat trip had taken him to New Orleans. But it was a big town to him.

He settled down in Springfield. He married Mary Todd—a clever, ambitious woman with a difficult temper. They had children, and he liked to play with the children—even when they scattered pens and ink all over his office. He became a well-known lawyer and on the whole a successful one. People knew he was honest—they called him "Honest Abe." They knew he would not plead a case unless he thought he had the right side of it. He was sent to Congress for one term, but he wasn't re-elected. "Too bad," thought his friends, "but—well, too bad." It seemed, for a while, as if he would end his days as a small-town lawyer, a local character, a teller of stories, a man of whom people said: "Well, you should have heard Abe Lincoln tell that one." And yet, all the time, he was walking up and down the streets of Springfield, in his rusty black clothes and his battered stovepipe hat where he kept his papers—driving in his buggy over the muddy, new roads of the state—wondering, thinking, questioning, being sad, and a joking companion, and a man who made hosts of friends, and a man who was hard to make out. The people who barely knew him called him "Abe" or, even in his forties, "Old Abe." His wife and his partner called him "Mr. Lincoln."

In 1854 or thereabouts, he was thinking, wondering—wondering about slavery, about the state of the Union. He had no personal or fiery hate for the slaveholders, but in a speech at Peoria he said: "Slavery is founded on the selfishness of man's nature—opposition to it in his love of justice." He let it stay at that, for the time. In 1858, a candidate for the Senate against Stephen A. Douglas, one of the best-known orators of the nation, he made his "house divided" speech. He and Douglas debated the question all over the states—the awkward, plain, backwoods lawyer against a speaker whom men called "The Little Giant." Douglas won the votes and went to the Senate. But Lincoln's words had sunk into men's hearts:

"All I ask for the Negro is that, if you do not like him, let him alone. If God gave him but little, that little let him enjoy."

"Our reliance is in the love of liberty which God has planted in our bosoms. Our defense is in the preservation of the spirit which prizes liberty as the heritage of all men, in all lands, everywhere. Destroy this spirit and you have planted the seeds of despotism around your own doors. Familiarize yourself with the chains of bondage and you are preparing your own limbs to wear them."

"It is the eternal struggle between two principles. The one is the common right of humanity and the other the divine right of kings. It is the same spirit that says, 'you toil and earn bread and I'll eat it. No matter in what shape it comes . . . it is the same tyrannical principle.' "

There was humor and satire, too. When someone held up a lantern to light his face on a dark night, he opened his speech by saying, "My friends, the less you see of me, the better you will like me." When he heard of a pompous man's impressive funeral, he drawled: "If General X had known what a big funeral he would have had, he would have died years ago." But the other words kept throbbing and burning in men's minds. Men were free—they ought to be free. Slavery was wrong. Democracy was a real thing, it could be lived. And so, at last, the new Republican party, vowed to certain frontier doctrines, to lands for the western men, to a hatred of slavery, met in convention and picked Abraham Lincoln as their candidate for president. After he was elected, he sold his house, tied up his trunks himself and addressed them "A. Lincoln, the White House, Washington, D.C." He said farewell to his old friends in Springfield. He was only fifty-one, but he said:

"Friends, for more than a quarter of a century, I have lived among you . . . Here I have lived from my youth till now I am an old man . . . Here all my children were born and one of them lies buried . . . Today, I leave you: I go to assume a task more difficult than that which devolved on General Washington. Unless the great God who assisted him shall be with me and aid me, I must fail . . . Let us all pray that the God of our fathers will not forsake us now. To him I commend you all . . . With these few words I must leave you, for how long I know not."

And what would happen now?

CIVIL WAR

The South had vowed that she would not accept a Republican president. South Carolina seceded from the United States on December 20, 1860. Alabama, Mississippi, Florida, Louisiana, and Georgia followed within two months. On February 8, 1861, representatives from the six seceded states met at Montgomery, Alabama, and formed the Confederate States of America. Texas joined them two weeks later. Lincoln was inaugurated on the 4th of March. He stated his position simply but firmly in his inaugural address: "In your hands . . . and not in *mine*, is the momentous issue of civil war. The Government will not assail *you* . . . But I hold that, in contemplation of universal law and the Constitution, the Union of these States is perpetual . . . No State upon its own mere action can lawfully get out of the Union . . ."

But, a little more than a month later, the first shots of civil war were fired, and four more southern states, Virginia, Arkansas, Tennessee, and North Carolina, joined the Confederacy. Thus begun, the war continued for four years. It was gallantly and bitterly fought. The men who died for the

South died, as they thought, for the independence their fathers had won before them. The men who died for the North died, as they thought, to preserve the Union their fathers had made before them. In all, according to the best estimates, 610,000 were killed or died of wounds and disease in the Civil War.

We could give a list of great battles—Bull Run, Chancellorsville, Antietam, Vicksburg, Gettysburg, Chickamauga. But that does not tell the story. The story was in the hearts of men and women—in the hearts of such men as Robert E. Lee, the great southern general, chivalrous, gentle, almost worshiped by his army and his people, who fought with dazzling skill to the bitter end and then accepted the fact of defeat with heroic courage and did all he could to lead and guide his broken land into paths of justice and peace—in the gay recklessness of the southern cavalry and the stubborn resistance of the Union soldiers that settled the issue at Gettysburg, the decisive battle of the war—in the hearts of innumerable, ordinary people, unknown to history, who suffered, endured, were brave, and made every sacrifice for the cause they believed in, on each side. But perhaps, it is better to repeat what Lincoln said, when he spoke at Gettysburg, to dedicate the graves there:

"Fourscore and seven years ago our fathers brought forth on this continent a new nation, conceived in Liberty, and dedicated to the proposition that all men are created equal.

"Now we are engaged in a great civil war, testing whether that nation, or any nation so conceived and so dedicated, can long endure. We are met on a great battle-field of that war. We have come to dedicate a portion of that field as a final resting-place for those who here gave their lives that that nation might live. It is altogether fitting and proper that we should do this.

"But, in a larger sense, we can not dedicate—we can not consecrate, we can not hallow—this ground. The brave men, living and dead, who struggled here have consecrated it, far above our poor power to add or detract. The world will little note, nor long remember, what we say here, but it can never forget what they did here. It is for us the living, rather, to be dedicated here to the unfinished work which they who fought here have thus far so nobly advanced. It is rather for us to be here dedicated to the great task remaining before us—that from these honored dead we take increased devotion to that cause for which they gave the last full measure of devotion—that we here highly resolve that these dead shall not have died in vain—that this nation, under God, shall have a new birth of freedom—and that government of the people, by the people, for the people, shall not perish from the earth."

Or to say what he said again in his second inaugural address:

"With malice toward none, with charity for all, with firmness in the right as God gives us to see the right, let us strive to finish the work we are in; to bind up the nation's wounds; to care for him who shall have borne the battle and for his widow and his orphan—to do all which may achieve and cherish a just and lasting peace among ourselves and with all nations."

For there breathes the American spirit, and it was in that spirit that Abraham Lincoln made war. And had he been permitted to make peace, he would have made it in that spirit. But he was shot by an assassin, ten days after the end of the war, on April 14, 1865, and died the following day.

REBUILDING

Now there was another task in front of the nation—a task of rebuilding, reconstruction, reconciliation.

The slaves of the South had been freed by Lincoln on September 22, 1862, when he issued a proclamation declaring that all slaves within any state or district then in rebellion against the United States should be, from the first of January, 1863, "thenceforward and forever free." And in 1865 and 1868, the Thirteenth and Fourteenth Amendments to the Constitution provided that "neither slavery nor involuntary servitude . . . shall exist within the United States, or any place subject to their jurisdiction" and that "all persons born or naturalized within the United States, and subject to the jurisdiction thereof, are citizens of the United States and of the state wherein they reside. No state shall make or enforce any law which shall abridge the privileges or immunities of citizens of the United States; nor shall any state deprive any person of life, liberty, or property, without due process of law . . ."

Human slavery, in the United States, was ended. The possibility of secession by any state and the splitting up of the United States into a lot of different republics was ended. Four years of war had settled those two questions. The nation, born in 1776, became one indivisible nation in 1865.

But many problems remained. The slaves, suddenly freed, became citizens without, in many cases, knowing much about the responsibilities of citizenship. The old plantation system of the South was wrecked and the South impoverished by the long years of struggle. Of the white leaders of the South, many were dead in battle, others took an oath of allegiance to a United States which they still felt to be their enemy.

If Lincoln had lived, there is no doubt that the whole problem of reconstruction and bringing the southern states back into the Union would have been more wisely and sanely handled. Instead, it was clumsily handled, on the whole, by vindictive men who wanted to punish the South more than they wanted to make a great country.

But this much may be said for the credit of Americans.

Again, there was no blood purge. There were no mass executions. No heads rolled.

The handful of fanatics who had plotted the assassination of Lincoln and other government leaders were executed. His actual murderer was tracked down and shot. The half-crazy officer who commanded a notorious southern prison camp was hanged. The former President of the Confederacy, Jefferson Davis, was kept for a while in prison with certain of his associates and then released. But that was all.

Not one of the great southern generals or statesmen—Lee, Johnson, Stephens, Hampton, Longstreet—was even tried for treason.

Lee's shining example in defeat was a model for all the South. He could have used his great name and fame in business. He could have written his memoirs and every southern family would have bought that book, if they had to starve to do so. But then he would not have been the man he was. Believing in education, as he had believed in it all his life, he became the president of a small southern college and performed his duties there with the tolerant patience and extreme devotion to duty that had guided him always. It was known as Washington College when he went there. It is now called Washington and Lee.

Rancor and bitterness remained. Injustices were done. For

a time, the South was under military government. The ex-Confederate soldiers suffered. The freed Negroes, suddenly thrust into freedom, suffered. They were preyed upon by rascals of both sides. Suddenly given the vote, they were allowed to form or to assist in forming state governments without any previous experience in self-government. It is hardly to be wondered at that these governments were corrupt, inefficient, and wasteful. They did pass many sound and progressive laws —but unscrupulous white men, carpetbaggers and scalawags, used the Negro legislators for their own profit, while the most responsible white men were forced to stand aside. Nobody had really thought the problem through. Such a condition would not last, and, by 1877, the governments of the southern states were again in the hands of white men.

Yet the Negro had been freed and was not to be pushed back into slavery. The South had been defeated in war, impoverished by the ruin of war, but the South was back in the Union. Men who had fought for the Confederacy were to become representatives, senators, governors of states. In the Spanish-American War, thirty-three years later, Fitzhugh Lee and other Confederate soldiers were to serve in the United States Army, and serve loyally and well. Even in the very beginning, as a great southern orator said, "As ruin before was never so overwhelming, never was restoration swifter. The soldier stepped from the trenches into the furrow . . . fields that ran red with human blood in April were green with the harvest in June." The nation had suffered a great and drastic shock, but it did bind up its wounds. In spite of all the mistakes, the fumbling, the faults of Reconstruction, a united people went forward.

AGE OF BRONZE, AGE OF LEAD

Went forward—but where?

That was the question asked by many of the best and wisest Americans and Europeans. It has been asked continually through American history. And it is being asked again today.

Where are you going? What are you about? Why are you doing what you are doing and what sort of thing do you expect to build in the end?

There is a typical American catchword: "We don't know where we're going, but we're on our way." And there is some truth in that, though only a half-truth. Americans are not particularly happy sitting still—they would rather be doing something, even if it is the wrong thing to do at the time. They would rather build something in the wrong place, at great trouble, and then have to tear it down again, once more at great trouble, than not build it at all. They have had contemplative philosophers, but they are not, on the whole, a contemplative people. They want to act and do. They want to get something done in a hurry and turn to the next thing. It is only when nothing gets done that they are really miserable. That is what really depressed them about the last Depression; for the first time in American history, nothing seemed to be going ahead. And always, they look to the future, to repay them for any mistakes of the past. And that gets them into a lot of trouble—and is their weakness and their strength. For they are fluid, not fixed, and always willing to learn and try. If they were suddenly given a complete and gold-plated Earthly Paradise they would at once set about trying to improve it.

The American dream had been many things—the fighting independence of the frontier, the Plutarchian free republic of the founders, the farmers' republic visioned by Jefferson, the frontier democracy of Andrew Jackson, the democracy of Lincoln who said: "As I would not be a slave, so I would not be a master. That is my idea of democracy"; the idea of selfless honor and selfless duty exemplified by Lee, the gay, lavish aristocracy of the well-bred, still within a republican framework and ruled by the code of the gentleman, that was the plantation system of the South at its best; the Puritan dream of New England, the plain living and high thinking of Concord—and the ten thousand dreams that flickered and died, the New Zions, the New Harmonys, the community experiments of every sort and shape from the phalansteries of Fourier to the religious experiment of the Shakers. For every possible way of living together has been tried in some part of America by people who wanted to try it—communism, socialism, polygamy, celibacy, planned genetics, rule by a prophet, rule by elders, guidance by spirits—everything. And, as long as these various experiments did not get in the way of the nation or in their neighbors' way, they were allowed to go on. There was enough room for them.

Now, however, for at least half a century after the Civil War, the American dream seemed to concentrate on three things—work, growth, money.

It was virtuous to work—the act of work was a virtue. It was virtuous to make money—men who made money were respected because they had made money. It was virtuous to do something big, build something big, in the terms of work and money—size in itself was a virtue.

Those who did not work and make money were idlers,

sluggards, and drones. They were not respected. Unless, of course, they could show that what they did had size or newness or marketable worth. An inventor like Edison was highly respected—there was the electric light that he had invented and you could turn it on and off. A thinker in mathematics and physics, like Willard Gibbs, was hardly heard of. The test of almost anything was "Will it work? Then how much is it?"

And, under this fierce, competitive, driving urge, great physical things were done and great projects achieved. The transcontinental railways were driven across mountains and deserts as if demons, not men, drove them on. Cities sprouted and grew where there had been no cities before. Whole forests were cut for lumber and floated down the rivers to the sawmills. The iron, the lead, the gold, the oil, the tin, the silver were dug and dragged out of the earth as if by a million trolls. The huge smelters and furnaces flamed through the night—by 1900 American furnaces produced as much steel as those of Great Britain and Germany combined. And with all this went constant invention, constant improvement of machinery—the telegraph, the telephone, the electric light, the Atlantic cable, the mechanical reaper, the harvester and thresher, the chilled-steel plow. Not all were American inventions, but any new invention the American could get his hands on he took, tried to improve, made in quantity, took a chance on it. It might be a pot of gold—anything from a city lot in Omaha to a safety pin might be a pot of gold. Oil, railroads, mines, machines, inventions—these made men rich. There were crashes and depressions, but they didn't matter—let's get going again and get on. Lose a fortune and make another—that was the American way. If Andrew Carnegie

makes four hundred million dollars out of his steel company
—bully for him! That shows what a poor, hard-working boy
can do. You've got to have a telephone and an electric light
and an automobile to be a good American—and if you don't
want them, brother, just move out of the way, for there are
lots of other folks that do. This is my busy day and no grass
grows on a busy street, and I'm not in business for my health.
Just look at the new opera house and the new rolling mill
and the new millionaire and the new university and the new
jail and the new stockyards—they're all bigger and better than
anything we ever had, and, if we don't like them, we'll tear
them down and build something bigger and better still. We're
busy—we're moving—we're hustling—we're getting up and
going—we don't know where we're going, but we're on our
way!

Now, of course, this wasn't all true—or even entirely true
of all Americans. But it was the keynote of the time. All
through it, a great many million people were living honestly,
soberly, quietly, in the fear of God and not in the worship
of money. All through it there were protesting and powerful
voices of Americans old and new who said: "This isn't what
we're really after. We want something better and more lasting than money and success." They ranged from Charles
Francis Adams, the great-grandson of the second President
to John P. Altgeld, the eagle unforgotten, who was governor
of Illinois and defended the rights of men to organize and
strike against the power of the Pullman Company, even
against the power of the federal government—and was hated
for it and maligned. But the rush, the roar, the building, the
money, the shouting of the big voices, set the tone of the
time. Even a man like Mark Twain, a magnificent and human

writer, who hated injustice, tyranny, and class distinctions, could spend years of his life and all his money on a type-setting machine that never succeeded in the end. Why? Well, being a writer wasn't quite enough—and he had an American fondness for machines—and, if he succeeded with the machine, he would be as much of a success as Clark or Tabor or any one of a dozen millionaires who had their small, garish day and passed.

Europe discovered something new—the American millionaire. He came to Europe with his pockets full of money and walked around looking at things, smoking cigars. He married off his daughters to penniless dukes and princes. He bought tapestries, paintings, statues, rare books, whole palaces, the worst art and the best art—but he bought. He supported art dealers, titled bankrupts, frauds, genuine artists, and people who made artificial wormholes in new furniture. He was caricatured, scoffed at, laughed at—but he paid cash. Often he was neither as much of a fool nor as much of a child as he looked—merely a busy man who had made a great deal of money and didn't know quite how to spend it but who had a vague idea that civilization was a good thing to buy, if you had the pocketbook. Sometimes, like J. P. Morgan, he knew very well what he was buying, often he did not. He was often cheated and fooled. But, in the end, what he bought came to America—and much of it, in the end, added to the enjoyment and benefit of the people.

For here came a curious extension of the American idea of hard work and money. The men who made the great fortunes—a good many of them—didn't find the making of those fortunes quite enough. Active during their working lives, once the pile was made they were unable to settle down and enjoy inactivity. The money worried them—for, if they knew nothing else, they knew that money was power. They had been born poor boys and plain citizens. They could buy European titles for their daughters, if they chose—there were no American titles that they could buy for themselves. And yet something had to be done with the money.

So we have Andrew Carnegie, with his fortune of four hundred millions, spending most of it to help found free libraries where boys who were as poor as he had been could get the books he had wanted to read when he was a struggling boy. We have John D. Rockefeller, who said of his money, "God gave it to me," founding the great Rockefeller Foundation, whose work in medicine and science has helped men everywhere. We have a family like the Guggenheim family, establishing a foundation which, every year, gives more than a hundred thousand dollars in scholarships to artists, writers, musicians, and scholars who have a job of work to do and need money to carry on the work. The masterpieces of art that Mellon and Kress bought are now in a public gallery where any American citizen can go to see them. The Morgan library, collected under the direction of J. P. Morgan and full of rare books and manuscripts, is now open to the public. It is a curious, interesting, and American phenomenon.

It is not necessary either to excuse or to apologize for the robber-millionaires of this period of American history. They existed, they cared little for the people, they meant to preserve their money and their status by fair means or foul. One of them said, "The public be damned"; another, now forgotten, referred piously to the businessmen in whose hands God had placed the destiny of the country. They were ruthless, acquisitive, selfish—and, in a few cases, men of far-reaching vision. The worst were thieves—the best gave money away, and money in millions, as skillfully and forehandedly as they had made it. And, out of all the noise and the turmoil, the great industrial plant of America got built. It was wastefully built, in money and human life, but it was built, and built at inconceivable speed. It concentrated great blocks of money and power in the hands of a few men—but the average standard of American living rose to a point not previously attained in the world's history. The average middle-class American lived better, ate better, had more things, and had more freedom of opportunity than most men anywhere.

Were the old American ideas—the ideas of the Declaration —lost and wiped out in this rush and press of building and money-seeking? They were not. Even in the eighties such men as Henry George, Edward Bellamy, and the first spokesmen of labor began to cry out against what they considered a danger to democracy. President Cleveland, in 1888, stated: "Corporations, which should be carefully restrained creatures of the law and servants of the people, are fast becoming the people's masters." William Jennings Bryan, in 1896, gained the Democratic party's nomination for president with a speech in which he said: "I come to speak to you in defense of a cause as holy as the cause of liberty—the cause of humanity. . . . The man who is employed for wages is as much a business man as his employer . . . The merchant at the cross-roads store is as much a business man as the merchant of New York . . . The farmer who goes forth in the morning and toils all day . . . is as much a business man as the man who goes upon the board of trade . . . the miners who go down a thousand feet into the earth . . . as much business men as the few financial magnates . . . Having behind us the

producing masses of this nation and the world . . . we say
. . . You shall not press down upon the brow of labor this
crown of thorns, you shall not crucify mankind upon a cross
of gold!"

Bryan, sincere but windy, more orator than thinker, was
beaten for the Presidency by the conservative and dull Mc-
Kinley. Nevertheless, he remained a force, and the best of his
words lived on. If there were men in America who thought
that the getting of money justified anything, there were also
many millions of ordinary Americans, living their daily lives
as good neighbors, proud of the freedom and the rights that
were their heritage, willing to admit any man or woman to
their company who showed himself honest, truehearted, and
decent in human relations, ready to stretch their hands to
the oppressed and the starving anywhere in the world. And,
if European visitors were often shocked and dizzied by the
clang of American industry, the corruption of American local
politics, the seeming worship of the dollar—they were also
impressed by the warmhearted friendliness of the average
American.

And still it was a name of freedom and that freedom
meant something—and perhaps that is the biggest and most
unrecognized fact of all. From 1860 to 1930, thirty-two million aliens came to the United States—and were absorbed into
the American system. Hungarians, Bohemians, Croats, Serbs,
Slovaks, Poles, Jews, Italians, Rumanians, Russians, Greeks,
Austrians, poured into the land. They came for the same old
reasons—liberty, opportunity, a chance for something better.
And some were fooled and coughed out their lives in tene-
ments, cursing the day—and some died in the steel mills and
were buried in cindery ground—and many found what they

looked for. We will not claim that all had an equal chance or the best of chances—millions came as cheap labor, drawn here by advertisements and circulars and agents who told them they might be millionaires, while instead they ground out their lives in the mills and the mines and the factories. But we will claim this—for we can—that to each new stock, the way of freedom was open. For some it was harder—yes. For some it was easier—yes. But Adamic, Pupin, Steinmetz, Riis, Lazarus, Knudsen, Cermak, Saroyan, are as American names as Adams, Brown, Smith, Douglas. They have made themselves American by their vigor, their talent, and their worth. They have enriched America by the gifts they or their fathers brought us from abroad. And they are part of our flesh and bone today.

RISE TO WORLD POWER

In 1898, the United States became a world power. Economically, industrially, it had been a world power long before. But with the Spanish-American War it took rank politically among the great powers of the world.

The ostensible reason for the war was the liberation of Cuba from Spanish domination and its immediate cause was the still unexplained blowing up of the American battleship *Maine*, in Havana harbor, killing 260 American seamen and officers. Americans felt their traditional friendliness toward any people in the Western Hemisphere who were trying to set up their own form of self-government—and Americans were deeply shocked and angered by the tragedy of the *Maine*. However, it is only fair to say that for many years there had been strong American sentiment for the annexation of Cuba, that American investment in and trade with Cuba had come to be important, and that a little more patience and tactfulness on the American side could have settled every point at issue between Spain and the United States without bloodshed. As it was, there was war.

Some fifteen years before, an American journalist had published a gloomy and prophetic article on just what would happen to the United States in the event of a war with Spain. This included the destruction of the American fleet, the shelling of New York, and the bombing of American cities by dynamite bombs dropped from balloons. But what was to happen was almost exactly the opposite.

The United States seemed very ill-prepared to fight a large-scale war against a European power. But, as it turned out, Spain was even worse prepared. The American Navy was a smart and efficient fighting force; the Spanish Navy, neglected and badly armed. At Manila and Santiago, the Spanish warships fought with all the courage that Spaniards have always shown in battle. But courage could not beat better gunnery. Two Spanish fleets were destroyed, with the loss of less than twenty men on the American side. At Las Guasimas, El Caney, and San Juan, Spanish soldiers fought with skill and heroism. But within four months the military and naval power of Spain had collapsed, and she had lost her last footholds in the New World.

It was the unexpected swiftness and conclusiveness of the American victory that surprised and astonished Europe. The United States was supposed to be a rich and thriving nation—but not a powerful nation in a military way. To put it crudely, the effect upon Europe was like the effect of a prize fight in which an unknown contender unexpectedly knocks out a champion. There was a new and incalculable force in world affairs.

What was the result on the United States and its citizens? The physical results were immediate. The United States acquired Puerto Rico. It acquired a protectorate over Cuba, subject to the resolution passed by the Congress when the United States entered the war that "The United States hereby disclaims any disposition or intention to exercise sovereignty, jurisdiction or control over the said Island, except for the pacification thereof, and asserts its determination, when that is accomplished, to leave the government and control of the Island to its people." It acquired Guam. And, for twenty million dollars, paid to Spain, it acquired the Philippines—and proceeded forcibly to annex them, against strong native opposition. At the same time, Hawaii voluntarily joined the United States.

From a country that had always said it wanted to be let alone by itself to work out its own particular destiny, the United States suddenly became a country with far-flung possessions and subject peoples. It looked like the start of an American imperialist system. And it was called just that— "American imperialism"—and not in praise—by the influential Americans who protested against the annexation of the Philippines as an act entirely contrary to American ideals. But the proof of the pudding is in the eating. Let us see how American imperialism worked out in practice.

In Cuba, as soon as the war ended, the military governor, General Wood, called a constitutional convention of Cubans to draw up a Cuban constitution. The constitution was adopted and Cuba became a republic, with its own president, vice-president, Senate, and House of Representatives. However, an amendment to the Constitution—the Platt Amendment, gave the United States the right to intervene to preserve Cuban independence and integrity. And, during the next twenty years, the United States did intervene, a number of times. But, in 1934, a new treaty with Cuba canceled the Platt Amendment and the United States no longer has the right to interfere in Cuban internal affairs. Economically and through the investment of American money in Cuban enterprises, Cuba is still strongly tied to the United States. Nor has this always been to the best advantage of the Cubans. But both republics look forward to a relation of increasing friendliness, and Cuban capacity for self-government has been well-established.

In Puerto Rico, the people have American citizenship and are governed by a legislature, elected by popular vote, and a governor appointed by the President of the United States. The economic problem of Puerto Rico is a difficult one and it cannot be said that the United States, in its position as guardian, has yet solved it. Nevertheless, education and sanitation have advanced, roads have been built, trade has increased, and a new generation of Puerto Ricans have had practice in helping to rule themselves.

In Hawaii, an act of 1900 gave full American citizenship to all former citizens of the kingdom of Hawaii, and Hawaii is ruled as a territory of the United States—a territory which may and doubtless will in time become a state of the Union. Hawaii is ruled by a legislature, composed of a House and a Senate elected by popular vote, and a governor appointed by the President of the United States. It sends a delegate to the Congress of the United States. A fertile group of islands, rich in tropical products and exquisitely beautiful, it can be fairly said that Hawaii is satisfied with the American way of government and looks forward to eventual statehood.

The Philippines present an unusual, interesting, and significant case. They were taken by force—there can be no doubt of that—and the Philippine insurrection against American rule lasted until 1902. But, under American rule, schools and roads were built, smallpox and cholera almost stamped out, the number of pupils attending school rose from less than five thousand in 1898 to nearly a million in 1920, the infant death rate in Manila was reduced from eighty to twenty per cent, and large estates were broken up into small farms that peasants could buy. The population of the Philippines was seven million in 1900, it is sixteen million today. In 1916, the United States pledged itself to withdraw from the Philippines, "as soon as a stable government should be established"; in 1934, the Tydings-McDuffie Act provided for complete Filipino independence after a ten-year transitional commonwealth government with a Filipino chief executive. The constitution of the Philippines adopted in 1935 provided for a president, a vice-president, a National Assembly—all elected by vote. Freedom of religion, the press, and right of assembly were guaranteed by the constitution. And, until the Japanese invasion of the Philippines, all these things had worked out. An enterprising, intelligent, and able people, always looking toward independence, had found certain definite benefits in United States rule but asserted their right to govern themselves—and the United States had freely granted that right. And, in the defense of the islands against Japanese attack, Filipinos and Americans fought side by side. Indeed, so united was that resistance that General MacArthur coined a word for it—"Filamerican." And today, the United States stands pledged to recover for the Filipinos that independence they have lost through no fault of their own, and to see to it that the flag of their commonwealth shall rise again over their islands, a flag of free, self-governing men and women.

Guam, Midway, Wake are United States naval bases in the Pacific. Those it has lost in battle, the United States means to recover, in battle. The Danish West Indies, purchased from Denmark in 1917 for $25,000,000, are now the Virgin Islands of the United States.

So much for American imperialism—an imperialism which has resulted in the Republic of Cuba, the Commonwealth of the Philippines, full American citizenship for the people of Puerto Rico, American citizenship and territorial status for the islands of Hawaii. It has not been always wise—it cannot claim to have lacked selfish interest. But it can claim to have brought to each new possession, or dependency, schools, modern ways of medicine, and practice in self-government. It has not said to any people: "You must stay the way you are. You must be our slaves." It has said: "Educate yourselves —learn how to govern yourselves. We don't want to keep on running things for you forever and ever—maybe we could, but it makes us feel uncomfortable. We believe in reading and writing—we believe in schools and hospitals—we don't believe in slavery, under the Stars and Stripes. We remember our own beginnings and our own hard road to independence. We would rather have free neighbors around us, helping us to work out in concert the problems of the Western Hemisphere, than vassal states."

Such has been the American doctrine; such, on the whole, has been American practice. We don't claim and we can't claim that we have committed no wrongs. No nation is spotless, and there are spots upon the shield of the United States. But every step forward toward the real sort of imperialism that sets out to crush and bind its neighbors has been followed by another step back. We have, at various times, sent troops into Haiti, Nicaragua, the Dominican Republic. And then we have called back those troops. During the period of the great revolution in our sister republic of Mexico, and the troubled times that followed that revolution, at one time American Marines were landed at Veracruz, at another time the raids of Villa across the American border brought an American expeditionary force upon Mexican soil. But what happened? Both expeditionary force and Marines came home again, having annexed and conquered nothing. There was no war with Mexico. Americans did not shout that they must have "living room" in Mexico or that Central America must be forced into an American "co-prosperity sphere." Dollar diplomacy, big-stick diplomacy died a natural death and were supplanted by the diplomacy of the good neighbor—the neighbor who wants to be a neighbor, not a master. And we mean to keep it that way. Today, the republic of Mexico, the republics of Central America, all but two of the great and powerful republics of South America stand by our side in this war. And they do so of their own free will.

The Panama Canal Zone is a strip of territory roughly forty miles long and ten miles wide, the "use, occupation, and control" of which the United States acquired by treaty from the newly organized Republic of Panama, November 18, 1903. We paid the Panamanian government $10,000,000 for it at that time, and after nine years started paying an annual rental, which today is fixed at $430,000. The governor of the Zone reports to the Secretary of War in Washington, and in time of war is always an Army officer appointed by the President.

The Canal itself, a magnificent and successful feat of engineering, links two oceans for peaceful trade and in time of war is a vital point in the naval defense of the United States. But it can hardly be denied that, in acquiring the Zone, the United States backed a revolution, if a bloodless one, against a weaker neighbor, the Republic of Colombia, and created suspicion and tension in Latin America. Once more, however, the years and the genuine American wish to be liked rather than feared by her neighbors brought about an adjustment of difficulties. In 1922 the United States paid $25,000,000 to the Republic of Colombia "to remove all misunderstandings" in connection with the revolt of Panama and the acquisition of American rights in the Canal Zone. And this payment marked a further shift in American policy from a temporary semi-imperialism of the early days of the century toward the policy of the good neighbor, the policy we carry on today.

That is the American record. We do not say that it is a perfect one. All we ask is that it be compared with the record of the Axis nations in their dealings with their own closest neighbors. Our tourists travel with handkerchiefs in their pockets, not with handcuffs for the souls of other nations. The idea of the master race—the master state—had never yet appealed to the American nation. And no man who ever believed in such ideas could guide and direct that nation of individualists.

THE AMERICA WE KNOW

From 1900 to the present, there has been a shift and a change in American life. There has been a struggle, too. The

"Square Deal" of Theodore Roosevelt, the "New Freedom" of Woodrow Wilson, the "New Deal" of Franklin Delano Roosevelt, all play their part in that struggle. It is partly the eternal struggle that goes on in any free nation—the struggle between conservative and liberal, between people who think that things ought to stay pretty much as they are and people who want reforms and changes, between men who think the people have enough power and men who think they should have more. But it has been the struggle of a nation still striving, still learning, still trying to find out not what works best for just one class of people, but what works best for all the people.

The significant thing about it has not been one law or another, not one president or another, but the struggle itself. For Americans may be anything you like, but they are not tame.

To the looker-on at the high tide of the nineties—that iron age of capitalism—it might well have seemed that it would go on unchecked till all the various trusts and combinations pooled quietly into one great supertrust and Mr. Billions ran the country. But that did not happen. No sooner did the new crop of millionaires and the great corporations seem firmly entrenched in power than people began to ask "Why?" "Why do children have to work in factories? Why can't workers organize if employers combine? Is making a lot of money the virtue we thought it for a while or is it just making money? Why aren't our city governments and our state governments better run? What's happened to the old American idea—the idea of small wealth and little poverty? What about this great industrial machine we're still making—what makes it run and who gets the profits and is the sharing fair?"

The people who asked the questions were called reformers, cranks, enthusiastics, long-haired idealists—but they kept on asking the questions. And out of their questions came many changes, experiments, reforms.

Here are a few things to remember about the United States.

Its big industries are not built on making a few expensive things for a few expensive people. They are built on making a great many things for a great many people and making them at a price that a great many people can pay. The real symbols of American industry are the Ford car, the dollar watch, the ten-cent can of soup, the cheap newspaper and free radio, the ready-made dress, the movie made at a cost of millions of dollars that you can see for forty-four cents. And into the making of all these things—and a million others—goes great skill and ingenuity. It has to, because, if the product isn't serviceable, Americans kick about it. They don't like cars that don't run and watches that don't tick and telephones and faucets that get out of order. They have been trained to expect convenience, ingenuity, and low price in the ordinary things they buy. They don't always get the best—a great many European products are more durable, beautiful, lasting than American products in the same field. But, because of mass production and mass buying, all sorts of things that make the life of the average family easier, pleasanter, and healthier are within that family's reach in America. American business sells to the many, it makes its money by selling to the many. It does so, of course, to make money. But, because it does so, the average standard of living has risen and is still rising. Americans still believe in an improvable future.

American society is still a fluid, not a fixed society, both in politics and business. The present President of the United States, Franklin D. Roosevelt, comes of an old American family, notable for service to the nation and comfortably well-to-do for generations. His Secretary of State, Cordell Hull, one of the most distinguished men in America, was born in humble circumstances ten miles from a railroad. His former Secretary of Commerce and present lend-lease administrator, Harry Hopkins, is the son of an Iowa harness-maker. The present Governor of Massachusetts, Leverett Saltonstall, is descended from Sir Richard Saltonstall, an English knight who came to the Massachusetts Bay Colony in 1630. The present Mayor of New York City, Fiorello H. La Guardia, is the son of an Italian bandmaster. Lieutenant-General William Knudsen, great industrialist, typically successful manufacturer, was born in Denmark. Felix Frankfurter, respected justice of the Supreme Court, was born in Austria of Jewish parentage. And we like that and we are proud of it. We want the United States to be a country where a man stands on his own feet, not just in his father's shoes—and where the gifts of a man can have full play. And it always has been that sort of country.

Americans believe in education. And they believe in free education, open to all who seek it, and in compulsory education up to a certain age. The schoolhouse is a typical American symbol, more typical than the battleship or the tank. There are more than 1,600 universities and colleges in the United States and in them, in 1938, there were 1,351,905 students. In 1940, the University of Michigan had over 13,000 students, the University of Illinois over 15,000. No, not all of these universities and colleges have the high standards or the old traditions of European universities. The pre-Hitler

German gymnasium, the French lycée, the schools of the Scandinavian countries had a thoroughness and a method unknown to many American schools. But from graduates of American colleges and universities, since 1930, have come three winners of the Nobel prize in physics, two in chemistry, two in medicine and physiology, three in literature. You will find Americans studying Homer in California, studying Racine in Kansas, studying Goethe in Pennsylvania. The American ideal is a completely literate nation, with higher education open to all who wish to take advantage of it. It has not yet attained that ideal. But it is moving toward it.

The United States has no military caste exerting political influence on national affairs. The officers of its Regular Army and Navy keep out of politics and have kept out from the first. No military coup d'état has ever been attempted by an American general or admiral in United States history. Candidates to West Point and Annapolis, the military and naval academies, are appointed from every state in the Union and have to pass a rigid, competitive examination before entrance. Neither blue blood nor money can buy a man's way into these academies and no political influence can keep him there if he fails to do well in his studies. The Army of the United States belongs to the whole nation and represents the whole nation. And its commander in chief is a civilian, the President of the United States.

Such are a few facts worth remembering about today's United States. We do not claim to have solved every problem before us—indeed, we know that we have not. For a long time, labor organization, labor laws, industrial regulation, safety regulations in industry lagged far behind those of Britain and those of many states in Europe. During the last thirty years or so, we have tried to close that gap, and we are gradually closing it. Our Social Security Act is not perfect, but it is in operation. Our labor organizations, grown vastly in the last ten years, are still in the testing crucible. But they are here to stay. Great inequalities of wealth and poverty exist. Not every American is well-paid, well-housed, well-fed. But we hope and trust in a future greater than our past—a future for the common man, who is our backbone and our strength and on whose possibilities for self-government, co-operation, and development our whole system is based. And we keep our rights as men.

We have not become—as some feared we might become—a nation ruled by wealth and devoted to gain. We have not become—as some feared we might become—an anarchical mob. Nor shall we in the future. For we do not sit down quietly and accept injustice and wrong. At no time has there been an abuse in America that has not been exposed, cried out against, attacked by free-speaking Americans. The progress since the first days of this century has moved in a jagged line of ups and downs, not a steadily ascending curve. But it has been progress. No sooner did vast concentrations of wealth seem to threaten the liberties of the common man than Theodore Roosevelt arose to denounce "malefactors of great wealth," preserve the public domain and propose governmental regulation of irresponsible industries. Woodrow Wilson, in his first inaugural address, said solemnly: "We have been proud of our industrial achievements, but we have not hitherto stopped thoughtfully enough to count the human cost. . . . The great Government we love has too often been made use of for private and selfish purposes, and those who used it had forgotten the people. . . . There can be no equality or opportunity . . . if men and women and children be not shielded in their lives, their very vitality, from the consequences of great industrial and social processes which they can not alter, control, or singly cope with. . . . I summon all honest men . . . to my side." And Franklin D. Roosevelt, in his first campaign for the Presidency, was to point directly to "the forgotten man, the man at the bottom of the economic pyramid" and insist that something be done to aid and help this man.

Nor were these words alone. They were followed by deeds and acts and laws to help and better the life of American citizens. The strain of idealism in the words—the search for a right and equal way of life—is neither a new nor a transient thing in America. Be not mistaken about that. It goes back to our deepest beliefs and our oldest traditions. It is part of the fiber of our minds and hearts. We shall make some silly mistakes on the way—Prohibition was one of them. But once we see a mistake, we remedy it. For, by long training in self-government, long practice of free speech and free religion, we have the power of self-remedy. And sooner or later it is always used, and the will of the people reigns.

AMERICA AND THE WORLD

Some pages back, we left the United States, for the first time recognized as a world power and making some tentative adventures in imperialism. We showed just what that imperialism amounted to as imperialism and how it worked out, not as a dictatorial American empire, resolved to extend its own boundaries and subjugate other nations, but as a system of dependencies and territories, each one self-governing, on its way toward self-government, or on its way toward full rights of statehood in the United States. It might be as well to add, at that point, that the United States had acquired no territory in continental North America since the purchase of Alaska from Russia in 1867, and that Alaska, now a territory, will eventually become a state of the Union. However, let us see what happened to the United States in relation to the rest of the world, and how that position has changed.

In the years from 1900 to 1914, certainly the last thing most Americans dreamed of was America's being involved in a war that started in Europe. The old idea and the old advice—to keep out of all European quarrels—were firmly fixed in the American mind. Not only did the United States wish no quarrel with any power either of Europe or of Asia—but the very idea seemed preposterous. Americans knew, when they thought about it, that the world had shrunk—that an ocean which had taken from six weeks to three months to cross in sailing ships could now be crossed in a week by a fast liner—that the cable, the telegraph were fast binding the far corners of the earth together. They knew that an epidemic, starting in Asia, might reach American shores and take American lives. They knew that their own trade spread out over the seven seas. They knew that famine in Asia, panic in Europe, had their effect on America. They knew that they were in more constant daily touch with all parts of the world than their fathers had dreamed possible. Yet they remained, for the most part, looking inward upon their own land rather than looking outward across the oceans. They were interested, as spectators, in events in Europe and Asia but these events did not touch them personally. The farmer in Kansas, the clerk in New York City, might read about coronations, earthquakes, revolts, discoveries across the water—but they were outside his own life. The recent immigrant might maintain a lively interest in the politics of his former homeland. But he was leading a new life and learning new ways—and, even to him, these were the important things.

The American knew as well that there were other governmental systems in the world besides his own—monarchies, limited monarchies, despotisms, republics. They were down in the history books he studied at school—now and then, from a fellow American or from travel, he learned something about them at first hand. But the fact that these other systems existed didn't trouble the average American. He might receive and welcome exiles from any oppressive political system. He might denounce the practices of Czarist Russia and hold meetings of protest against pogroms. He might sympathize with small nations oppressed by great ones and he might, and often did, fight as a volunteer for the small against the great. He would and did give money, food, medical supplies, and every sort of aid to the homeless and hungry three thousand miles away. But politically he was willing to let other nations go their own ways as long as they let him go his. He hoped that, in time, these other nations would adopt democratic systems similar to his own—it would, to his way of thinking, make a more liberal and better world. But he didn't mean to force his own democratic ideas down the throats of other nations.

That is a fair statement of the average American attitude of 1914. It may seem a naïve and provincial point of view, but it was a genuine one. And then things began to change, very rapidly.

At first, and again to most Americans, though not to all.

the First World War in Europe was something they read about in the newspapers. They did not think it could affect them. They picked one side or the other, as one picks sides in a game between two teams—a bloody game and a horrible game, but a game played out by foreigners. America's strong link with Britain—a link made of speech, culture, books, ideas shared in common—inclined many Americans toward the side of the Allies. America's historic friendship with and respect for France played its part. But there were millions of Americans, also, whose forebears had come from Germany—the old Germany of great music and great science. They mightn't think much of the Kaiser and their fathers might have come to America for a freedom they could not find in Germany—but the ancient ties were strong.

Gradually, inexorably, the situation worsened. American ships were sunk by German submarines, American citizens killed and drowned. The United States government made strong protests to the governments of both Great Britain and Germany as to their conduct of the war and how it affected American rights. But one icy fact remained. Great Britain's conduct of the war killed no Americans. Two hundred and nine American lives were lost on the high seas by German action.

Nevertheless, America wished to keep out of the war. President Wilson bent his every effort to that end. He appealed to the warring governments for peace—he offered to mediate between them in any way possible. It was useless. And the Imperial German government decided upon unrestricted submarine warfare. As we know, from since published books, this was a deliberate act on the part of the German government. They were willing to risk war with the United States on the chance of crushing their opponents before the United States could bring its full weight to bear on the other side.

The challenge was now direct and the danger immediate. It is true indeed and it will always remain true that the United States cannot, for its national security, afford to have the Atlantic Ocean controlled by any unfriendly and aggressive power. But this was not what moved the hearts of most Americans in 1917. They saw the honor of their country assailed, the flag of their country fired upon without cause, their liberties in danger. "With a profound sense of the solemn and even tragical character of the step I am taking and of the grave responsibilities which it involves, but in unhesitating obedience to what I deem my constitutional duty," declared President Wilson to the Congress of the United States on April 2, 1917, "I advise that the Congress declare the recent course of the Imperial German Government to be in fact nothing less than war against the government and people of the United States . . . But the right is more precious than peace, and we shall fight for the things which we have always carried nearest our hearts—for democracy, for the right of those who submit to authority to have a voice in their own governments, for the rights and liberties of small nations, for a universal dominion of right by such a concert of free peoples as shall bring peace and safety to all nations and make the world itself at last free."

The government and people of the United States. That was what they fought for.

You know what happened then. Unprepared—not half as prepared as we were at the start of the present war—we put more than 2,000,000 Americans soldiers into France. American industry and American manpower were mobilized. "America," said the German general, Ludendorff, "thus became the decisive factor in the war." And the war ended with the complete defeat of Germany and her allies.

We had our losses as well—bitter losses in dead and wounded. We spent both blood and treasure. We got no territory. The only territory we got in Europe is the six feet of ground apiece in which our dead soldiers sleep—and even that ground is not ours. The money we spent was spent—never fully to be repaid. But we had fought for the things we believed to be right—and neither the cost nor the effort was grudged by the American nation.

The President of the United States, Woodrow Wilson, had had a great and mighty dream of the future. He dreamed of a League of Nations, a World Court, a system of world co-operation that should, as he said in his war message, "bring peace and safety to all nations and make the world itself at last free." He set down Fourteen Points that might bring about world peace:

I. Open covenants of peace, openly arrived at, after which there shall be no private international understandings of any kind but diplomacy shall proceed always frankly and in the public view.

II. Absolute freedom of navigation upon the seas, outside territorial waters, alike in peace and in war, except as the seas may be closed in whole or in part by international action for the enforcement of international covenants.

III. The removal, so far as possible, of all economic barriers and the establishment of an equality of trade conditions among all the nations consenting to the peace and associating themselves for its maintenance.

IV. Adequate guarantees given and taken that national armaments will be reduced to the lowest point consistent with domestic safety.

V. A free, open-minded, and absolutely impartial adjustment of all colonial claims based upon a strict observance of the principle that in determining all such questions of sovereignty the interests of the populations concerned must have equal weight with the equitable claims of the government whose title is to be determined.

VI. The evacuation of all Russian territory and such a settlement of all questions affecting Russia as will secure the best and freest co-operation of the other nations of the world in obtaining for her an unhampered and unembarrassed opportunity for the independent determination of her own political development and national policy and assure her of a sincere welcome into the society of free nations under institutions of her own choosing; and, more than a welcome, assistance also of every kind that she may need and may herself desire. The treatment accorded Russia by her sister nations in the months to come will be the acid test of their good will, of their comprehension of her needs as distinguished from their own interests, and of their intelligent and unselfish sympathy.

VII. Belgium, the whole world will agree, must be evacuated and restored, without any attempt to limit the sovereignty which she enjoys in common with all other free nations. No other single act will serve as this will serve to restore confidence among the nations in the laws which they have themselves set and determined for the government of their relations with one another. Without this healing act the whole structure and validity of international law is forever impaired.

VIII. All French territory should be freed and the invaded portions restored, and the wrong done to France by Prussia in 1871 in the matter of Alsace-Lorraine, which has unsettled the peace of the world for nearly fifty years, should be righted, in order that peace may once more be made secure in the interest of all.

IX. A readjustment of the frontiers of Italy should be effected along clearly recognizable lines of nationality.

X. The peoples of Austria-Hungary, whose place among the nations we wish to see safe-guarded and assured, should be accorded the freest opportunity of autonomous development.

XI. Rumania, Serbia, and Montenegro should be evacuated; occupied territories restored; Serbia accorded free and secure access to the sea; and the relations of the several Balkan states to one another determined by friendly counsel along historically established lines of allegiance and nationality; and international guarantees of the political and economic independence and territorial integrity of the several Balkan states should be entered into.

XII. The Turkish portions of the present Ottoman Empire should be assured a secure sovereignty, but the other nationalities which are now under Turkish rule should be assured an undoubted security of life and an absolutely unmolested opportunity of autonomous development, and the Dardanelles should be permanently opened as a free passage to the ships and commerce of all nations under international guarantees.

XIII. An independent Polish state should be erected which should include the territories inhabited by indisputably Polish populations, which should be assured a free and secure access to the sea, and whose political and economic independence and territorial integrity should be guaranteed by international covenant.

XIV. A general association of nations must be formed under specific covenants for the purpose of affording mutual guarantees of political independence and territorial integrity to great and small states alike.

In regard to these essential rectifications of wrong and assertions of rights, we feel ourselves to be intimate partners of all the governments and peoples associated together against the imperialists. We cannot be separated in interest or divided in purpose. We stand together until the end.

For such arrangements and covenants we are willing to fight and to continue to fight until they are achieved; but only because we wish the right to prevail and desire a just and stable peace such as can be secured only by removing the chief provocations to war, which this program does remove. We have no jealousy of German greatness, and there is nothing in this program that impairs it. We grudge her no achievement or distinction of learning or of pacific enterprise such as have made her record very bright and very enviable. We do not wish to injure her or to block in any way her legitimate influence or power. We do not wish to fight her either with arms or with hostile arrangements of trade if she is willing to associate herself with us and the other peace-loving nations of the world in covenants of justice and law and fair dealing. We wish her only to accept a place of equality among the peoples of the world, the new world in which we now live, instead of a place of mastery.

Neither do we presume to suggest to her any alteration or modification of her institutions. But it is necessary, we must frankly say, and necessary as a preliminary to any intelligent dealings with her on our part, that we should know whom her spokesmen speak for when they speak to us, whether for the Reichstag majority or for the military party and the men whose creed is imperial domination.

We .have spoken now, surely, in terms too concrete to admit of any further doubt or question. An evident principle runs through the whole program I have outlined. It is the principle of justice to all peoples and nationalities, and their right to live on equal terms of liberty and safety with one another, whether they be strong or weak. Unless this principle be made its foundation, no part of the structure of international justice can stand. The people of the United States could act upon no other principle; and to the vindication of this principle they are ready to devote their lives, their honor, and everything that they possess. The moral climax of this the culminating and final war for human liberty has come, and they are ready to put their own strength, their own highest purpose, their own integrity and devotion to the test.

Wilson was not the only man to dream of such a world. Other men had dreamed of it before and were dreaming of it then. The common people of many nations dreamed of it and wished for it. And it could have been made.

Why it was not made would take too long to tell here. We cannot go into all the bargaining and disputes of the Versailles Conference—we cannot go into all the reasons for that failure. If you wish to say that the United States was partly or even largely to blame for that failure, we shall not dispute you. Woodrow Wilson, an idealist, a dreamer, a great man, had neglected certain practical aspects for the fulfillment of his dream. He had not called the leaders of the opposite party in the United States into conference with him and assured their co-operation. He had not sufficiently explained to the American public their true interest in such a world league. Small and selfish men defeated America's participation in the League—and broke Woodrow Wilson's heart. He died a martyr, not just to his own ideas, but for every man everywhere who wishes peace, security, and liberty. Yet, before he died, he said a word on his own defeat and failure: "I am as sure of the ultimate triumph of our cause as I am sure that God reigns."

After Wilson's fall from power, American "isolation" bloomed again—for a while. And the planes grew and the planes flew—and the distance of earth shrank like drops of water in summer. The United States was still anxious for peace. In 1921, she initiated a disarmament conference. In 1928, she initiated the Kellogg Pact, condemning recourse to war on the part of nations. But the planes grew and the planes flew—and systems that could not bear liberty trampled on the rights of man and began to grow and wax stronger in the Axis countries.

With the rise of Nazism in Germany and the growth of a ruthless and aggressive military party in Japan, it became more and more evident that the United States faced its gravest crisis since 1776. The dictatorial thrust of the Axis countries was a thrust that affected all men, everywhere. They said and meant that they intended to be masters of the whole world. They said and meant that they intended to set up master races and subject races. They could not—and said they could not—afford to let the United States remain an island of liberty in an enslaved and darkened world. And Americans, whatever their defects, have a certain amount of common sense. They know slavery when they see it; they know dictatorship and hate it; they know threats and will not suffer them. And they are a fighting people.

So now we, the United States, are once more at war. Treacherously attacked by the Japanese at Pearl Harbor—threatened, wheedled, and attacked by Germany, Italy, and their allies—we are once more at war. And let no man mistake this. That war will be fought to a finish. Every resource of the entire industrial plant of the United States—all the fighting manpower the United States can call to the colors—is being brought into action. If it should take years of struggle—if it should require such sacrifices from American citizens as have not been known in our history—we will fight this war till the governments of the Axis countries are crushed to the earth, their dictatorships abolished from the memory of man, and their military and naval power completely and utterly destroyed. For, as we could not live in a country half slave and half free, so we cannot live in a world half free and half slave.

Those who oppress their fellow man today will not always oppress him. Already they stand on the edge of a gulf and their armies march to destruction. Already the quicksand has taken hold on their feet and the noose for their necks is weaving. They have boasted themselves invincible and all-conquering—already it is later in the day than they think, and they have but little time left for the boast and the tyranny. The free men are on the march—the United Nations are marching

—the morning star of freedom gleams in the sky. Let those who would compromise with tyranny and slyly seek for a hiding place in tyranny's bosom do so—they do so at their peril, for they will have to answer for it sooner than they know. But let all who love liberty and cherish peace and fair dealing join hands with us, for they shall be as welcome to us as if they were brothers in blood.

AND AFTER THE WAR

We have tried to show, in this little book, something about the sort of people we are—something about the United States, what it believes in, how it grew, what ways of life it follows. We have not told all our history, but we have not glossed the record. We have put down faults as well as merits. We have done our best to tell the truth about the things we believe.

There remains one question—and a big one—which must be in all our minds and perhaps even more in the minds of outside nations. What does the United States *want*, once the United Nations have won their inevitable victory over the Axis? What are its aims, its intentions, its goals for a future world?

The United States does not want world empire. It does not want subject peoples. It does not want to be a master race. All these ideas are utterly and completely opposed to the American idea, the American way of life, and the history and development of the American people.

It does not want an inch of ground in Continental Europe. It does not intend to expand its own direct rule anywhere in the Western Hemisphere. It does not wish to exercise economic dominance over any other nation, anywhere. Pending the establishment of a true world peace, it must keep and maintain such air bases as are vital to its national defense and national security. But its aim in so doing will be peace, not war. For the United States wants peace—and not a peace of the dead, but a peace of the living—not the peace of a jail, but the peace of a world of free men. It believes in the dignity and the worth of man, it believes in the building of the great house of mankind.

It has stated its basic ideals for the world that will rise from this war, in the Four Freedoms—freedom of speech, freedom of worship, freedom from want, freedom from fear. Not just for United States citizens. But for all men, everywhere.

In concert with Great Britain, it has already set forth certain principles in the Atlantic Charter. That Charter reads as follows:

"The President of the United States of America and the Prime Minister, Mr. Churchill, representing His Majesty's Government in the United Kingdom, being met together, deem it right to make known certain common principles in the national policies of their respective countries on which they base their hopes for a better future for the world.

FIRST, their countries seek no aggrandizement, territorial or other;

SECOND, they desire to see no territorial changes that do not accord with the freely expressed wishes of the peoples concerned;

THIRD, they respect the right of all peoples to choose the form of government under which they will live; and they wish to see sovereign rights and self-government restored to those who have been forcibly deprived of them;

FOURTH, they will endeavor, with due respect for their existing obligations, to further the enjoyment by all States, great or small, victor or vanquished, of access, on equal terms, to the trade and to the raw materials of the world which are needed for their economic prosperity;

FIFTH, they desire to bring about the fullest collaboration between all nations in the economic field with the object of securing, for all, improved labor standards, economic adjustment and social security;

SIXTH, after the final destruction of the Nazi tyranny, they hope to see established a peace which will afford to all nations the means of dwelling in safety within their own boundaries, and which will afford assurance that all the men in all the lands may live out their lives in freedom from fear and want;

SEVENTH, such a peace should enable all men to traverse the high seas and oceans without hindrance;

EIGHTH, they believe that all of the nations of the world, for realistic as well as spiritual reasons, must come to the abandonment of the use of force. Since no future peace can be maintained if land, sea or air armaments continue to be employed by nations which threaten, or may threaten, aggression outside of their frontiers, they believe, pending the establishment of a wider and permanent system of general security, that the disarmament of such nations is essential. They will likewise aid and encourage all other practicable measures which will lighten for peace-loving peoples the crushing burden of armaments."

The Atlantic Charter is not a Ten Commandments or a final pronouncement. But it shows clearly enough that co-operation among nations, not conquest of other nations, is the goal of the United States.

The Vice-President of the United States, Henry A. Wallace, has already said, of the peace to come: "The peace must mean a better standard of living for the common man, not merely in the United States and England, but also in India, Russia, China, and Latin America—not merely in the United Nations, but also in Germany, Italy, and Japan.

"Some have spoken of the 'American Century.' I say that the century on which we are entering—the century which will come out of this war—can be and must be the century of the common man. Perhaps it will be America's opportunity to suggest the freedoms and duties by which the common man must live. Everywhere the common man must learn to build his own industries with his own hands in a practical fashion. Everywhere the common man must learn to increase his productivity so that he and his children can eventually pay to the world community all that they have received. No nation will have the God-given right to exploit other nations. Older nations will have the privilege to help younger nations get started on the path to industrialization, but there must be neither military nor economic imperialism. The methods of the nineteenth century will not work in the people's century which is now about to begin. India, China, and Latin America have a tremendous stake in the people's century. As their masses learn to read and write, and as they become productive mechanics, their standard of living will double and treble. Modern science, when devoted wholeheartedly to the general welfare, has in it potentialities of which we do not yet dream."

This new world can be made. It cannot be made by the Axis powers—it is not the world they want. It cannot ever be made by the Axis powers—they live by war and fear. It cannot ever be made by the Axis powers—they make science itself the tool of war and fear, not the servant of peace. But, in the United States, we think of science always as the servant and strong right arm of peace. Already and even under the stress of war, our scientists are developing new and undreamed-of gifts that will serve and help mankind. They can do so because they are free men—free to think and look ahead.

We call to our side all free men and women everywhere who will help us to make that world. We call to our side all those who sorrow and are oppressed. We call to our side all those who hate tyranny and fight it. We call to our side all those who want to see their children free.

The enemy has said that this war decides man's fate for the next thousand years. We accept that challenge. Behind us lie three hundred years of history—three hundred years of belief in liberty and the rights of man. That belief is no idle dream—it has made us great among the nations. We cherish it, we thrive by it, we live and die by it. We shall fight for it to the end. And that fight we know how to wage. We have the machines and the men, the brains and the skill and the strength. We have the food and the steel, the oil and the metals. If we have to build a hundred thousand planes a year, for victory, we shall do so. If we have to train every citizen in arms and the making of arms and the trades that back up armed might, we shall do so. If we have to invent more appalling instruments of destruction than the world has yet seen, we shall do so. For this is a finish fight and we mean to finish it—and finish it in such a manner that our children and all children shall be free from the shadow of tyranny and the threat of new world wars.

That is what we are after, that is what our flag means. It means freedom and it means hope. It means a good neighbor, not a master. It means men making their own destinies and running their own government. It means peaceful men who can fight with God's own wrath in them when their country is assailed. It means a nation and a people who believe in man and man's future and the free world that man can make.

Listen once more to the voices—the voices of past and present, speaking the American dream:

Our fathers were Englishmen which came over this great ocean and were ready to perish in this wilderness; but they cried unto the Lord and he heard their voice and looked on their adversity. Let them therefore praise the Lord . . . let them which have been redeemed of the Lord, show how he hath delivered them from the hand of the oppressor . . . Let them confess before the Lord his loving kindness and his wonderful works before the sons of men.

William Bradford, 1647

In the name of God, amen. We, whose names are underwritten . . . do, by these presents . . . covenant and combine ourselves together in a civil body politick . . .

The Mayflower Compact, 1620

. . . shall have and enjoy all liberties, franchises and immunities within any of our other dominions, to all intents and purposes as if they had been born within this, our realm of England . . .

The Virginia Charter, 1607

The sovereign, original and foundation of civil power lies in the people—people may erect and establish what form of government seems to them most meet . . .

Roger Williams, 1644

The doctrine in persecution for cause of conscience is most evidently and lamentably contrary to the doctrine of Christ Jesus, the Prince of Peace.

Roger Williams, 1644

The Public must and will be served.

William Penn, 1693

Is life so dear, or peace so sweet, as to be purchased at the price of chains and slavery? Forbid it, Almighty God! I know not what course others may take; but, as for me, give me liberty or give me death!

Patrick Henry, 1775

We hold these truths to be self-evident, that all men are created equal, that they are endowed by their creator with certain unalienable rights, that among these are life, liberty, and the pursuit of happiness. That to secure these rights, governments are instituted among men, deriving their just powers from the consent of the governed . . .

The Declaration of Independence
Thomas Jefferson, 1776

Observe good faith and justice toward all nations. Cultivate peace and harmony with all . . .

Farewell Address
George Washington, 1796

Equal and exact justice to all men, of whatever state or persuasion, religious or political; peace, commerce and honest friendship with all nations . . . freedom of religion, freedom of the press, freedom of person under the protection of the habeas corpus and trial by juries impartially selected . . . these principles form the bright constellation that has gone before us and guided our steps . . .

First Inaugural Address
Thomas Jefferson, 1801

In charity to all mankind, bearing no malice or ill-will to any human being, and even compassionating those who hold in bondage their fellow men, not knowing what they do . . .

John Quincy Adams, 1838

By the rude bridge that arched the flood,
Their flag to April's breeze unfurled,
Here once the embattled farmers stood
And fired the shot heard round the world . . .

Ralph Waldo Emerson, 1836

They are slaves who fear to speak
For the fallen and the weak;
They are slaves who will not choose
Hatred, scoffing and abuse
Rather than in silence shrink
From the truth they needs must think;
They are slaves who dare not be
In the right with two or three . . .

James Russell Lowell, 1843

God grants liberty only to those who love it and are always ready to guard and defend it . . .

Daniel Webster, 1834

Justice is the great interest of man on earth . . .
Daniel Webster, 1845

I leave this rule for others, when I'm dead. Be always sure you're right, then go ahead.
David Crockett, 1834

Government is a trust, and the officers of the government are trustees; and both the trust and the trustees are created for the benefit of the people . . .
Henry Clay, 1829

Our reliance is in the love of liberty which God has planted in our bosoms. Our defence is in the preservation of the spirit which prizes liberty as the heritage of all men, in all lands, everywhere.
Abraham Lincoln

Government of the people, by the people, for the people shall not perish from the earth . . .
Abraham Lincoln, 1863

I shall fight it out on this line if it takes all summer.
Ulysses S. Grant, 1864

I hear America singing, the varied carols I hear . . .
Walt Whitman

Thunder on, Democracy . . .
Walt Whitman

Liberty is to be subserved whatever occurs . . .
Walt Whitman

The United States themselves are essentially the greatest poem . . . Here at last is something in the doings of man that compares to the broadcast doings of the day and night . . .
Walt Whitman, 1855

Public officers are the servants and agents of the people, to execute the laws which the people have made . . .
>
> Grover Cleveland, 1882

There must be, not a balance of power, but a community of power; not organized rivalries, but an organized common peace . . .
>
> Woodrow Wilson, 1917

America lives in the heart of every man everywhere who wishes to find a region where he will be free to work out his destiny as he chooses . . .
>
> Woodrow Wilson, 1917

We maintain and defend the democratic form of constitutional, representative government . . . Through it we can obtain a greater security of life for our citizens and a more equal opportunity for them to prosper . . . through it we can best foster commerce and the exchange of art and science between nations . . . through it we offer hope for peace and a more abundant life to the peoples of the whole world . . .
>
> Franklin D. Roosevelt, 1936

The four freedoms . . . freedom of speech, freedom of worship, freedom from want, freedom from fear . . .
>
> Franklin D. Roosevelt

Praise the Lord and pass the ammunition! . . .
>
> American song, 1942

That is what we say. That is what we mean. That is how we grew. That is what we are. Those are the things we believe. That is America.